Venus

To Sam and Alicia, who were
born during the writing of this book

Published by
Arcturus Publishing Limited
1–7 Shand Street, London SE1 2ES

This edition published 2001

ISBN 1-84193-052-0

Typography by Alex Ingr
Cover design by Chris Smith

Printed and bound in Malta

Venus

*How to discover the spirit of
love in everyday life*

WILLIAM WRAY

ARCTURUS

Contents

Introduction

The birth of Venus

Any time that is not spent on love is wasted.
TASSO

O F ALL THE POWERS which dominate our hearts and minds, none is more deeply sought after nor more deeply missed than love. We yearn for love.

We long to receive love, and we long to give it. Much of our frustration in life – our sense of sorrow and loss, our sense of inadequacy, the lack of faith in ourselves and mistrust in the circumstances with which we are presented – arises from a disconnection with this principle of love. Consider those things which give profound satisfaction, and you will find that they arise out of love and are fed by love. When we stop to ponder on what is of central importance to us, what lies behind any satisfaction we might derive from life, without which we lack direction and certainty, when we consider what we derive our happiness from, the inevitable conclusion must be that it is love.

Love goes by many names, but what in essence is this love which all of us desire, and from where does it arise? Certainly the objects of love appear beyond us, but love is experienced within, and in love's expression – that which is within is given to that which is beyond. See a baby smile and you'll know what I mean. In their smiles babies give themselves totally. Where do babies learn such things?

We may appear to be particular and separate from all else, but the central issue in our lives knows no such division. It was there from the beginning, and though we may be able to carry on without it, and some may argue that by necessity we must, lack of love leaves its mark. If you are in any doubt about this, look at what has motivated men and women since the beginning of time. Look at those who have lived full and useful lives and those who have destroyed themselves. Better still, look to your own life. Look at those things that make us mean and small and those things that encourage evolution and expansion. Love finds its expression in many ways, but there is at the heart of all our enthusiasms a love for the things we lend ourselves to.

Love is a principle of profound importance. It is not something that requires intellectual endeavour. The lover knows more about the ultimate nature of things than those who pride themselves on their analytical minds, unless they too are lovers in disguise. Love is immediate and of the essence of things. Love is the blood of life and, though it may be mangled out of all recognition, it lies at the heart of things.

If this is to be really known as a fact of life, a powerful presence in our thoughts and deeds, we have to devote ourselves consciously to the principle of love. We must become lovers, but not those of the acquisitive kind. To possess love is an impossibility: love is a universal principle and knows no bounds, and, knowing no bounds, it cannot, therefore, be contained. However, there is a substratum of ourselves which lies beneath all our thoughts and feelings. This is the ground of love, and learning how to gain access to it and release its power is the key to human happiness.

Love is the gift of oneself, and in giving we receive. Love is the true price of love, and, therefore, if we wish to receive love, we must first find the means of giving it. In giving love we learn more about it, and in learning more about it we learn more about our own essential selves.

The purpose of this book is to explore this central issue in our lives, to devote ourselves to it, not wait for love to make an occasional appearance but to transform our lives by living in its memory. We will learn to explore its domain and to encourage its presence. We will consider what others have discovered on the way of love, reflect upon their discoveries and apply them to our own situation in the most practical way. However, before we do, let us first look more closely at the nature of love and the guises in which she appears to us.

Love is a Goddess

Love is a goddess who goes by many names. The Greeks called her Aphrodite, the Romans Venus, and it is by these two names she is most widely known.

Of all the philosophical works that have made their mark over the centuries, Plato's *Symposium* still holds its preeminence. It is a discussion of the nature of the love we yearn for.

If our understanding of life is to reach its proper fullness, if we are to experience the great richness of life, then a proper understanding of love must be our aim. We, like Plato and those other ancient philosophers, must explore love and enter into a deeper relationship with what I shall call the Venus Principle. Venus must become central to our thoughts and deeds.

In the ancient world the goddess of love was spoken about, remembered, evoked. Her presence at any feast of those who wished to explore life's significance was considered to be a necessity.

It was felt that, without her finding her proper place, our experience of life must by necessity become empty, directionless and disillusioned. For them Venus is the fire which ignites the human spirit, that arouses devotion, that sets us all on a path of fulfilment. She is the soul's central principle. Without service to the spirit of love, without the Venus Principle featuring in some way in our lives, the lack of direction and disillusion of which so many complain must be everyone's personal experience.

To discover how we too might consciously recognize, understand and honour this abiding principle of love in our lives, and how we might serve her in all her many manifestations, is a matter of genuine consequence and severe practicality. Our task is not only to discover the importance of a devotion to the spirit of love, but how it might be used in our direct experience of life.

We have physical organs that can be cared for and maintained in a proper state of fitness. We also have subtle, inner organs which need to be cared for so that they too might serve the human purpose. This is not just a matter of encouraging mental facility, for it also includes the whole emotional realm, the heart as well as the head. The great Platonic philosophers had no doubt that love leads all the way on the path of human fulfilment. They were also certain that the organs of insight needed to be tended, developed and utilized to the full if this journey were to be undertaken.

Our task is to discover the nature of Venus, to explore what habits of heart and mind we should develop in order to confirm the existence of love within us, and go on to allow her presence to inform our choices, stimulate our creativity and illuminate our experience of life.

To help in this undertaking, the sections of this book will be divided into two aspects: thought and reflection followed by practice. The practice arises directly out of the thought and reflection. The two go together. The application of ideas is all-important. You can read as many books of advice as you like, but it is the practical application of theory which proves whether the ideas are valid or not.

Before there can be the birth of Venus there must first be a period of pregnancy, and nobody ever got pregnant theoretically.

The Real Venus

We all have a rough idea as to who Venus might be. She has an insistent sort of presence which commands attention. There are plenty who have auditioned for the part and many who have attained the status of an icon by embodying something of her magic. Those who spring most immediately to mind are women, and certainly the myths related to Venus show her as all-woman.

But she is not just the preserve of women. All of us have the power to love. We neglect love at our peril, man or woman. The one thing that destroys more completely than the passion of unmeasured love is the suppression of love.

During the Florentine Renaissance there arose a love for the classical world, and much of human understanding was brought to light. Men of wealth sent their servants far and wide in a determined attempt to discover yet more neglected Greek and Roman manuscripts left rotting in obscure monasteries, and scholars devoted themselves to learning classical Greek in order to translate these works. The endeavours of these individuals changed everything. Of all the treasures they unearthed and translated the dialogues of Plato became of preeminent interest, especially *The Symposium*. This work was the one most read, most renowned and of most influence, and not only amongst the learned, the men of letters, poets or educated courtiers. It found its way into the streets by way of the public theatres to become part of a general way of thinking.

At the heart of the great flowering of the arts, the rebirth of culture that we associate with the Italian Renaissance, lay a concept of overriding importance. This idea was, needless to say, derived from *The Symposium*. The Platonic writers of the Renaissance gave it a name: 'platonic love'. Even today the term is sometimes used, usually to describe that kind of relationship which people really believe is platonic in name only. In truth 'platonic love' has a far deeper significance than we would ever imagine.

Not one Venus but twins

Although it goes by his name, 'platonic love' is not the sole preserve of that most influential of all philosophers, Plato, or indeed of his teacher, Socrates. It is an eternal and universal principle which is the fundamental property of every individual. It is as close as life itself. But for it to fully manifest it must be properly understood, served and used in the practical affairs of life. The

Florentines did so. The fire of love they lit produced some of the greatest works of art the world has known. Their discoveries totally transformed our view of ourselves. At the heart of it all was the principle of love.

One of the most famous of all Renaissance paintings is Botticelli's *Birth of Venus*. Why is it one of the most well known and well loved paintings of all time? Because people cannot help but respond to its timeless beauty.

In it the heavenly Venus is seen on a scallop shell riding naked across the sea towards the land. The sea is her element, for according to legend she is born of air and water. On the left of the painting, Zephyrs, the winds of spring, blow her towards the shore on the right. As she approaches land, Flora, the goddess of nature, is preparing to clothe the naked goddess in a cloak embroidered with the beauties of nature.

The heavenly Venus was born of Uranus without a mother, but the earthly Venus had both, being born of Jupiter and Dion. The fact that she has no mother indicates that in her heavenly shape there is nothing of the material about her. In myth, mother symbolizes the field of materiality. In her material form, however, she is born from the womb of her mother, Dione.

Each Venus has its own kind of innate love. The heavenly Venus loves to contemplate the beauty of its own fundamental being, whereas the material Venus is 'entranced by procreating that same beauty in bodies'.

We are touched by the influence of Venus in both her aspects. One draws us into a full and creative relationship with the fascinating forms of this world, the other to the love that lies at the very heart of things. If we were today to make a full and practical connection with this abiding principle in her double form, it would transform our lives. Our task will be how, in the most immediate and practical way, this might be achieved, and how we might fall in love with the unified beauty of love?

Why do we long for love yet abuse her?

At the heart of everything we do is the search for love. Love is what turns survival into life. Without being moved by love, life loses its true significance.

The principle of love is at work from our conception, in our birth, in the care that is granted us by home and family, in our desire to seek our destiny in the world, in the friendships we forge, in the experiences we share, in the desire to create our own families. Interpreted in this way, Venus is none other than the desire which both leads us to search for our own totality and the joy that is experienced when a sense of that discovery is made. This process lies at the heart of every creative act.

And yet if Venus is so all-powerful, what is it that, so much of the time, makes us not only ignore her power but often deliberately work against it? What is it that causes us to destroy rather than create? What makes us work towards suppressing her expression rather than assisting in the creativity of love? Perhaps worst of all, what makes us abuse her power?

Our task in pursuing Venus through the pages of this book is to discover not only something of her potency but also those habits of mind we adopt that prevent her proper expression, to find them and transcend them.

The light of love

The philosophy of love offers an alternative to those many schools of psychology that have tended to teach that neurosis is caused by the suppression of desire. According to the philosophy of love the neurosis we experience arises out of a lack of self-knowledge.

What in fact is being suppressed is a deep yearning to experience the truth, a personal truth, the truth about ourselves. Traditional wisdom states that the truth we are yearning for is to be found in the love that links us to the totality of human experience at the very deepest level.

Around this need everything in the human psyche is arranged, like planets around a sun. Unless we attend to that luminous centre of love, our experience must be affected by a sense of division and separation. And if this is how we experience things as an individual, it must also affect our experience of family and of society.

As a clear indication of this we need only look at the current state of the family, for what manifests on an individual level must by necessity move out into the widening spheres of human relationships at every level. The obvious need for the individual, the family and the nation is for division and separation to give way to connection and communion. The social disharmony and general fragmentation we encounter in so much of society is not so much an indication of the lack of love, more its malformation.

The strange thing about love is that it can easily manifest as hate. It all depends upon the limits we lay upon ourselves. Very often we try to create some kind of limited sphere at the centre of which we live and over which we try to exert a controlling influence. Into this sphere we draw all the things we hold dear: wealth, fame, pleasure, power. These things we try to manipulate in order to serve whatever end is ruling our minds. If this is how we function in life, if this is what we love, then very quickly will come anger and deceit. When anger and deceit become the primary power, true love makes a rapid departure. When love departs, the happiness we were seeking in all our schemes goes with it. What we are then left with is fear, fear of being thwarted, fear of seeing all our plans come to nothing, fear of being deprived of our pleasures, fear of being left alone and ignored, fear of death and oblivion.

Love, the expression of unity

When a child is hurt he turns to his mother for comfort, for the healing power of love. He does not need to think about it. Love is sown into the set up, and to be separated from it is to be truly cast out. The child turns to his mother in order that what lies within him may find expression. Compassion on one side gives comfort on the other. They are two aspects of the same uniting principle. A child, by turning to the healing power of his mother, is expressing the unity of love. A mother, by taking a child in her arms, is expressing the same. They are acknowledging the presence of a principle that is not just locked into their own separate psyches, for at that moment mother and child are subsumed by love.

When we look at the fundamental human relationships, we find the same thing. On the individual level we experience a relationship individually, but when the power of love arises, either consciously or unconsciously, the individual gives way to the universal. The desire to communicate, join in, come to an understanding, share and express, all these are but some of the continuing declarations of the same eternal principle.

But may we claim the right to have love on demand? Is understandable damage done when we react to our frustrated demands?

Questions of this nature must necessarily arise from an individual point of view. When the circle expands no further than the individual, these must be pressing questions. It is a kind of thinking and feeling which is based on duality. We are laying down a dividing line. On one side of this dividing line is me, and all the world from which I might draw the things which will satisfy my desires lies on the other side.

In addition, out there are all the things that might threaten what I believe I possess. The me-and-the-world approach that starts in duality can so easily end in fear, loneliness, and total separation.

Happiness becomes our substantial experience when the principle of unity, the principle of love, becomes the fundamental reference for our thoughts and deeds, when the principle of love expands beyond our limits to include an ever-widening circle of care and compassion.

No one ever loved separately

As no one ever loves separately, we must be on the look out for that 'state' and re-educate our minds to think differently. Loneliness takes many forms. We may be surrounded by company and still live in isolation. But for some there is no dividing line. We must learn to see the circle of limitation and transcend it: open our hands, open our hearts, give what we lack. When the circle is transcended, everything is experienced differently. We step out of that enclosed place, and knowledge, compassion, courage and love are found where fear once ruled.

Our task is to rediscover what was once perfectly natural to us, the capacity for love. And not just love up to this point and no further, for love by its very nature has no limit. In the discovery of love's limitless nature resides all that allows humanity to make true connection and evolve.

As Venus is unrestrained, she must be ever expansive.

As love is to be discovered at no time except in the present, then Venus is ever new. There is no such thing as an old love. When things are new, you see them afresh. When they are seen afresh, new and creative approaches become possible. It is no longer a matter of doing your best within the limits you have imposed upon yourself at some time in the past. It is a matter of constantly expanding those limits, reaching out, discovering more. And in reaching out and discovering more, there comes inevitably a greater depth of understanding. One learns more of the depth of love as well as its extent.

The source of inspiration

Poets and philosophers have constantly referred to the transformative nature of love. Even when their poetry is tinged with melancholy, it is because they are separated from the joy of love that is the source of their inspiration.

But whenever there is an expansion of consciousness, whenever new knowledge is discovered, sorrow is shrugged off, fear is abandoned and joy is found. No one expressed the nature of this transformation better than Shakespeare. In the following sonnet, for instance, he starts by describing a familiar condition. He is outcast and alone.

> *When in disgrace with Fortune and men's eyes,*
> *I all alone beweep my outcast state,*
> *And trouble deaf heaven with my bootless cries,*
> *And look upon myself and curse my fate,*

How familiar is this state: alone, separate, filled with regret and dismay, and, following on from that, a feeling of self-pity. But out of this inevitable sequence of emotion comes a sudden change.

> *Yet in these thoughts my self almost despising,*
> *Haply I think on thee, and then my state,*
> *(Like to the lark at break of day arising*
> *From sullen earth) sings hymns at heaven's gate,*
> *For thy sweet love remembered such wealth brings,*
> *That then I scorn to change my state with kings.*

Such is the power of love. The last lines of his poem describe the opening of the heart, the movement away from what the poet describes as 'sullen earth' – the experience of life we have when locked into a state of separation – to an experience of union with his beloved. The day breaks and in the morning sun he expresses his joy even at 'heaven's gate'. Such is the power of love, and such is the force of its expression.

This sonnet describes in metaphorical terms the soul rising from division and disappointment to discover its true 'state'. It describes a psychological transformation. This transformation accompanies the movement out of self-imposed limitation into a wider and more illuminated state of love.

This experience of universal love is not just the preserve of the poet. Einstein expresses the nature of this unconfined state and what he considers our task to be:

A human being is part of the whole, called by us 'Universe', a part limited in time and space. He experiences himself, his thoughts and feelings as something separated from the rest – a kind of optical delusion of his consciousness. This delusion is a kind of prison for us, restricting us to our personal desires and to affection for a few persons nearest to us. Our task must be to free ourselves from this prison by widening our circle of compassion to embrace all living creatures and the whole of nature in its beauty.

This is an expression of platonic love. Einstein is not the only lover to be found amongst the 20th century's leading physicists. Their quest for deeper understanding inevitably led them to the domain of love. Consider these words by Max Planck, the formulator of quantum theory:

Science enhances the moral value of life for it furthers a love of truth and reverence – love of truth displaying itself in the constant endeavour to arrive at a more exact knowledge of the world of mind and matter around us, and reverence, because every advance in knowledge brings us face to face with the mystery of our own being.

In his reflections about the nature of science, Planck expresses thoughts that have been formulated over and over again. It is an entirely natural process that the beauty he sees in the lawful expression of the manifest world draws him to both acknowledge and express the love that lies at the very heart of our being. These are the twin Venuses expressing themselves through his penetrating and inspired research.

Transcending the limits

We need to find a practical expression of love within the context of our own lives, and so transcending the limits is our task also. This needs to be done in the way we play our individual parts in life, in the way we meet the events that arise for us personally. It is for us to widen our circle of compassion, to meet all situations in the spirit of love, seeing the evidence of Venus in the unfolding world before us and acting from that knowledge. We can only do this when we transcend limits. When love is locked within limits it becomes bound. When it transcends limitations it is free.

Only if a particular limit or circle is transcended would the substance of love be experienced differently. In the bound state we experience fear and all that follows from it. Through true love, the realm of knowledge, compassion, mercy and joy would form the basis of our experience.

We would as individuals not only witness the birth of Venus but also be part of its ever-expanding world. Our task is to consciously connect with that world in order to play our full and creative part.

This is our birthright and yet it is so often denied to us. In this there is a terrible irony, for we are the cause of our own deprivation. Venus, however, is born continuously. Being an eternal principle it is ever new. Each new moment, therefore, provides its own opportunity. Our task is to recognize this fact in experience and be in at the birth.

The birth of love

This is where we begin – now. Although we may in our exploration ask the advice of those who have gone before, the journey is ours, and it is one that only we as individuals can undertake; each one of us will make our own discovery.

But let's not forget that love is a universal principle, and, in as much as each of us makes our own individual quest, so the principle of love will become more accessible to everyone. In our time we are locked into a way of thinking that insists on a kind of individuality that leads to separation, but love by its very nature connects, combines, unites. The soul is far greater than the individual body.

Our task is a simple one: to learn more about the presence of

Venus, magnify her presence by consciously devoting our actions to her and then pass on her presence, which we can't but do if we have faith in her existence.

To assist in this, the book has been deliberately designed so that there are things to think about, reflect upon and put into practice. If it achieves what it sets out to do, to bring about the birth of Venus, then it must, above all, encourage practice. The gods don't come unless invited. Nobody ever learnt to love in theory. Reflect upon the thoughts contained here and try to apply the practices that are to be found at the end of each section. Be experimental in your approach. You might like to read the book in its entirety, conscious of how it develops, step by step. Or you might like to use it as a means of personal exploration, taking each section as something to be used on one particular day, returning to those aspects which are of particular importance to you. But, whichever way you choose, there is much here to discover.

Let's begin.

Chapter one

Acknowledge the presence and create the forms

C ONSIDER THOSE PEOPLE you have come across who encourage your admiration by the way they take on the business of life. Because their sphere of influence may be small, these people will escape the notice of history. They do, however, have their own power.

Take, for instance, a beautiful woman I once knew. Her name was Jesse. She lived in the Dee Valley in North Wales with her children and grandchildren. The family ran a small pub called the Sun Inn. Jesse did the cooking and arranged the flowers that adorned the bar. She would go out walking in the lanes, picking the flowers from the hedgerows and arranging them as she walked along.

When she returned to the pub, she would take a vase and simply drop the flowers in, and because of her love for the flowers, they appeared to be in total accord with her wishes and fell into place. The whole thing was settled in one simple gesture, and there appeared an arrangement, entirely artistic and utterly natural.

Everything about her had the sense of ease and contentment. Her life was rich, and everybody loved her. There are people like this, who appear to be effortlessly and unselfconsciously in touch with the divine powers, rooted in themselves and at ease with the world.

I met her thirty years ago, and yet her memory remains, vividly alive long after she died. Did she think of herself as anything exceptional? I doubt it. Yet she lives on in the memory of a person whom she met for a few days long ago. In the course of time all memory of her will pass, but the qualities she embodied will never die. She was a perfect example of somebody who acknowledged the presence and created the forms.

PRACTICE

- When next you meet somebody you really admire, consider exactly the qualities that person possesses. If some time later that person should disappoint you, recall the qualities you originally saw in them.

Possessing the magic

Now, how do we possess ourselves of some of the magic that seems to come so effortlessly to these people? All of us are capable of transforming situations, if we knew how, and making something appear as if out of nothing. This operates in all spheres.

Take, for instance, a friend of mine who is the owner of a successful business. She runs this business from her home. Recently she was involved in negotiations with a much larger company. Things were not going well. As the negotiations progressed matters got worse and worse until they were all but deadlocked. Concern for the situation, fears about the outcome, doubts about her own capabilities, dominated her mind.

It was suggested that it was time to adjourn the meeting. When the others had gone, she looked back over the situation with a heavy heart, and was about to sink into a state of dismay when she decided not to follow that road.

Instead she fell still, came completely to rest, and put aside all concerns relating to her situation. From a deeper aspect of mind the thought arose of something we had been discussing a few days previously, the principle of beauty. She went out of her office, where the meeting had been held, and into her dining room. She took a vase and arranged some flowers. She gave the task her full attention. She saw the flowers, their individual beauty and the beauty of the completed arrangement. When she had done this she placed the vase on the table. When the meeting was reconvened, she suggested that they move out of the office into the dining room.

Everything changed. The matters that had caused so much concern were resolved without too much difficulty and entirely to her satisfaction. An understanding was reached. As her new business partners left, they suggested that in future all meetings should be held round the dining room table.

When encountering difficulties, it is often helpful to stop worrying at them. Learn to use the reflective powers of the mind, and between action let there be reflection. This is the way of allowing the Venus Principle to inform events.

There is a calm region within us all, and this is the source of true creativity. By going to that place, you are attuning yourself to a greater depth within yourself. Even if you feel you have gone entirely off track and have been swallowed up in a welter of events, this kind of attunement can be achieved through practice and effort. You may not make the connection immediately. Give it time, but only time enough. The needs that you have to meet are present, and you must learn how to meet them beautifully, now. Acknowledge the presence and create the forms.

PRACTICE

- Acknowledge the presence and create the forms by creating something beautiful.
- What you do may be something as simple as tidying your desk.
- Don't think the situations you are meeting fail to warrant the effort – every situation creates its own opportunity.

Socrates acknowledges the presence

At the beginning of Plato's *Symposium*, the narrator, Appollodorus, describes how after guests of the playwright Agathon had gathered at his house, preparing themselves to enjoy a dinner party, they suddenly realized that the guest of honour, Socrates himself, wasn't present. A servant was sent to look for him. He returned and informed the others that Socrates had retired into the portico of a nearby house: 'There he is fixed and when I call him he will not stir.'

Agathon insisted that he should be called again but was encouraged to leave him alone, being assured that Socrates made a habit of going off anywhere he happened to be and falling into states of abstraction.

Given that their symposium was to be devoted to a discussion of the nature of love, how appropriate that Socrates should take time to reflect before events got underway. It is difficult to speak of love if the beloved hasn't first been called to mind.

PRACTICE

• Before racing on to the event to come, still the mind and take time to reflect. It may only be a moment, but that moment provides an opportunity for you to come to yourself.

The source of creativity

There is no doubt that Shakespeare was one of the greatest of all creative geniuses. What he had to say about the creative act must therefore be taken with some seriousness. His work embodied the spirit of Venus. When the final curtain has fallen on any of his great works, you may discover something that has been there all along but unnoticed beneath the play of character and events. This elusive substratum provides the audience with the satisfaction that always accompanies great art. It is something more than all the elements from which the play is made. It is the source of his genius, the place from where it all arose, the depths of Shakespeare's mind.

What is to be found at the source of his genius?

In *Love's Labour's Lost* – a play in which, after the labour is over the true nature of love is found – these strict words are spoken to the aspiring poet:

Never durst poet touch a pen to write until his words were tempered with love's sighs.

According to Shakespeare, only by acknowledging the presence of love can there be any hope of fulfilling the poet's true role.

When you are in love, it is very easy to acknowledge the presence of love. Anybody who has ever felt the pangs of love will have no hesitation in confirming this. With this acknowledgement tempering his words, the poet, according to Shakespeare, creates something which 'would ravish savage ears' – still the most passionate movements of mind – and 'plant in tyrants mild humility'. His words are coming from a place that is beyond all that, beyond passing passion, beyond the demands of the ego. It is from here that his creativity arises. When he asks for 'the muse of fire' to 'ascend the brightest heaven of invention', Shakespeare is asking to be taken to that place where true inspiration arises.

PRACTICE
- Every time a good idea or apt response pops into mind, just before you claim it as your own, pause for a moment to wonder where it came from.

Something out of nothing

In *A Midsummer Night's Dream* Shakespeare says this of the creative act:

The poet's eye in a fine frenzy rolling doth glance from heaven to earth, from earth to heaven and as imagination bodies forth the forms of things unknown the poet's pen turns them to shapes and gives to airy nothing a local habitation and a name.

He speaks as a lover empowered by the spirit of love, creating works that are timeless in their beauty and wisdom. The fact that his poetry speaks to the human spirit as forcefully now as it did when it was written, despite the radical changes in the way we view ourselves and the world in which we live, indicates the power of that connection.

There is no doubt as to what he devoted his genius: the spirit of love. Inventive power is a most remarkable thing. From the individual's point of view it appears to be the capability of creating something out of nothing, and that which seemed inconceivable is formulated and brought to fruition by the employment of this power. Out of 'airy nothing' something appears.

Any of us who have made a sudden insight into the way things are, or have in a moment realized how best to meet a pressing need, know what it is to create something out of nothing. The answer is simply there. It may seem the obvious thing, but it is only obvious because of the perfect fit it makes to what is being presented. You can be sure that the more sense there is of a perfect fit, the greater the part love plays in the whole process, and the more love is allowed to play its part, the greater the sense of satisfaction.

I have a friend who, being taller than most women, found it very difficult to find a perfect fit. She therefore decided to meet an obvious need, and now has a chain of 25 shops, called Long Tall Sally. There are more tall women than one might imagine. When I asked whether she enjoyed the business, she said, 'I love it.'

PRACTICE

- The perfect fit can only be found by giving attention to the present need.
- Embrace the present. Enter it with enthusiasm and, if you lack enthusiasm, give what you lack.

The perfect hit

One of the most noticeable things about the music of Mozart is the sense of perfect fit, the sense that it would be impossible to add or take away a single note. It was as if the music in all its perfection simply poured out of him. In one of his letters Mozart describes the act of composition and the deep satisfaction that follows from it:

When I am, as it were, completely myself, entirely alone and of good cheer – say, travelling in a carriage, or walking after a good meal, or during the night when I cannot sleep; it is on such occasions that my ideas flow best and most abundantly. Whence and how they come I know not; nor can I force them. Those ideas that please me I retain in memory, and am accustomed, so I have been told, to hum them to myself ... Provided I am not disturbed my subject enlarges itself, becomes methodized and defined, and the whole, though it be long, stands almost complete and finished in my mind, so that I can survey it like a fine picture or beautiful statue, at a glance, nor do I hear in my imagination the parts successively, but I hear them as it were, all at once. What a delight this is I cannot tell you!

Here is a description given by a man who lived on intimate terms with harmony, and there is no doubt that love informs the whole process. Nor is there any doubt as to the effect. The pleasure of hearing the beauty of those freshly created forms provides its own joy. A close friend of Mozart said this about his creativity:

Sometimes he spent the whole night at the piano, for these actually were the creative hours of his heavenly ideas ... Whoever heard Mozart in such hours alone knew the depth, the vast extent of his musical genius.

PRACTICE

- Like Mozart's friend, listen with full attention to a piece of music that gives you real pleasure and ask yourself where you have been taken by that music.

Why make the effort?

It is evident that creativity of this nature is accompanied by a great love for the act of creation and a willingness to pursue an insight regardless of the time taken or sacrifice involved. For Mozart and Shakespeare it all appeared so easy. A connection was made and works of sublime beauty appeared. For others the task is much more demanding, requiring years of work to bring it to fruition. The original insight may appear in a moment, but then follows a prolonged period of exploration. Einstein worked on what became known as the 'theory of relativity' for many years after an insight into what the world must look like travelling at the speed of light. The way for Einstein may have been long and arduous, but love was still the driving force.

This can be easily seen when Einstein speaks of the work of Max Planck:

The longing to behold harmony is the source of the inexhaustible patience and perseverance with which Planck has devoted himself to the most general problems of our science, refusing to let himself be diverted to more grateful and easily attained ends. I have often heard colleagues try to attribute this attitude of his to extraordinary will-power and discipline – wrongly in my opinion. The state of mind that enables a man to do work of this kind is akin to the religious worshipper or the lover; the daily effort comes from the heart.

The way Einstein speaks of a scientist for whom he evidently feels great fondness is indicative of what he himself faced, pursuing with the same resolution matters to which his heart and mind were also devoted. Notice that it is his own idealism that enables him to recognize the idealism with which another eminent scientist was willing to pursue ends that were ultimately demanding, rather than going after easier options. Here are two men who were willing to persevere in the face of difficulties, their work arising just as much from the heart as the head. This is Venus operating in a field not usually associated with her realm.

These are people with great gifts, but what of the rest of us who do not possess their gifts? The first thing to recognize is that we all have our role to play, a role which is ours alone. We can play this part beautifully with heart and mind in exquisite accord, or we can ignore the opportunity, be careless of our talents, refuse to recognize those things to which we would love to devote ourselves if only we had the conviction.

PRACTICE
- Think about what it is you devote yourself to, and then go on to ask yourself what more you might offer.

This is the process

To do things out of love is a freeing way to act. Acting just for the love of it is a wonderful way of stepping free from the enthralling nature of action. So easily we are bound by what we want and what we don't want, desperate to attain, fearful of failing. Success and failure will come. Learn from them both. Use your willpower and continuous activity. Refuse to submit to failure, but also don't be seduced by success. Devote the whole of your willpower to mastering one thing at a time.

There is a process that you can follow:

PRACTICE
- Choose your task.
- Concentrate on a single purpose.
- Turn to the calm region of the mind.
- Open your mind to all possibilities.
- Wait for a clear course to be suggested.
- Use all the force of your will to accomplish your objective.
- Love doing it by doing it for the love of it. This will naturally arise if what you are doing meets a genuine need, and it will meet a genuine need if the Venus Principle is uppermost in your mind.

Facing failure

We are driven by the need for success and then cast down when success doesn't seem to come. All of this consumes a tremendous amount of energy. Energy in any event is naturally employed in the actions of the body. In addition, energy is required in all the processes of thought, emotion and will. But nothing exhausts energy faster than fear.

If failure comes, avoid being sucked into a state of self-recrimination. Disengage your emotions. Look coolly at the factors that caused the failure in order to avoid the same mistake again. Be in no doubt that without an intelligent appraisal and some self-analysis the same thing will happen over and over again.

What matters is not so much what comes to pass, but how you meet those passing events. If you operate from a state of total involvement, you disengage from the eternal principles and lock on to the inconstant and changing. Perpetual restlessness conquers peace of mind and inner happiness. Under such circumstances there is no hope that you might learn something from your experience.

PRACTICE
- When failure appears to overwhelm you, remember to give your attention to the need in hand rather than dwelling on your sense of failure.
- Concentrate your thoughts.
- Overcome restlessness of mind and fall still.
- Come into the present.
- Recognize the presence of love which sustains all that lies before you.
- Remember that failure also comes to pass, that in the movement of events something that seems to be of huge consequence will in time disappear into obscurity.

Setting course

Marcus Aurelius, who was both a philosopher and a ruler of the Roman Empire, faced on a daily basis responsibilities that most of us can only dimly imagine. There were plots, feuds, insurrections and threats of invasion, as well as great triumphs, plans for public works, and the laying down of a legacy that formed so much of civilization as we know it in the West. So what, when meeting the challenges of defending the Roman Empire, did he consider to be the primary question? In his Meditations, he made this remarkable observation:

How is my soul's helmsman going about his task? For in that lies everything. All else, within my control or beyond it, is dead bones and vapour.

Here, as far as he is concerned, is the key question when meeting his responsibilities, when encountering success and failure. What was important was not to be found in the realm of political action or speech making; action he called 'dead bones' and oratory, 'vapour'. For him the important issue was the source from which outer events arose, where his discrimination guided his heart and mind. The rest was merely the result of that inner connection.

Another of his reflections gives a clear indication of where he wished his soul's helmsman to guide him, to the port of inner connection:

Men seek seclusion in the wilderness, by the seashore, or in the mountains – a dream you have cherished only too fondly yourself. But such fancies are wholly unworthy of a philosopher, since at any moment you choose you can retire within yourself. Nowhere can a man find a quieter or more untroubled retreat than in his own soul; above all, he who possesses resources within himself, which he need only contemplate to secure immediate ease of mind. Avail yourself often then, of this retirement, and so continually renew yourself.

Understandably enough, he must have entertained the desire to get away from it all, to walk in the mountains, to wander by the sea shore, to escape the constant demands of his public life, but these desires he dismisses as unworthy of a philosopher.

There is another resource more immediately to hand, an inner world of stillness and rest. He speaks of 'inner retirement', connecting with the source of things that lie beyond the welter of events, the screaming demands. But this is not just a refuge, a place to escape to. It is more a place of renewal, a place from which he might return to the fray with renewed creative energy.

PRACTICE

- Consider, like Marcus Aurelius, how your soul's helmsman is going about his task, so that when the demands of life seem intolerable, you too may consider what is of real importance and by so doing find your inner sanctuary.

We too are actors on the world stage

If there was ever an actor on the world stage it was Marcus Aurelius, but we are all actors on the world stage. When we think of the great movements in society, the rise and fall of civilizations, we are looking at the effects of the thoughts and deeds of individual human beings.

If, when considering our own part in life, this is too epic a view, consider the role we play at work, within the context of the family, out and about with friends, and we will find that, like any actor, we have to learn to play our parts beautifully. But an actor has to retire behind the scenes to change his costume and renew his inspiration. He can not be forever 'out there'. After a long run, any play inevitably gets tired. Means have to be discovered to tap the source of creativity anew in order to keep things fresh.

The kind of renewal Marcus Aurelius is speaking about is always immediately to hand. He is speaking of that place where Venus dwells. The world of divine principles is always new. That is why these principles are considered eternal. They are not eternal because they have been around for a very long time. They are not subject, as we are, to the realm of time, the duality of past and future. They are constant in the constant present, and in going to that place where we might meet them, we are freeing ourselves from the fears for the future and regrets about the past. We are entering the eternal present. It is a way of freeing ourselves from the pressure that locks us into a cycle of stress.

The stresses that went with being the ruler of the Roman Empire are hard to imagine. This must have been especially so for somebody with a proper understanding of his responsibilities and a determination to fulfill them to the uttermost of his abilities. A lot was at stake. But Marcus Aurelius had a resource that he turned to over and over again. In his Meditations he encourages others to do the same. 'Avail yourself often.' That means not just the occasional recourse.

PRACTICE

- Turn to the spirit of love within yourself. Make it your source of thought and action.
- To help you in this, carry with you something you really love. Turn to it over and over again to remind you of the nature of love.

Finding something that suits you

In this book you will be offered many ways of changing habits of mind, stepping over impediments and making connection with the profound principles that are being considered. This, hopefully, will not stop you making your own creative approach. How to do this will be different for each one of us. We all of us need to find our own way, and that way will be dependent upon our circumstances.

A senior executive spoke recently of how he had adopted such an approach. Previously he had taken as a virtue the practice of mixing freely with his staff. He was rarely in his office. He made himself constantly available. This he considered good practice, and he took it up with some enthusiasm.

The only problem was that he found the whole thing exhausting. The demands of the job had to be dealt with, and so had the demands of those with whom he worked. The demands of his staff were often coloured by personal considerations, ideas about themselves and their position in the company. He found all this tended to cloud his judgement.

He decided to take a different approach and to spend a certain amount of time each day in his own room. He would ask people in one at a time and discuss with them individually the issues concerning them. Between each interview he would fall still, open his mind and reflect for a few moments. He said that working in this way made it so much easier to attend to exactly what was arising in the present, to identify the real issues and separate them from matters coloured by personal considerations. In this way, clear and intelligent decisions could be reached.

PRACTICE
- Consider your own situation and be inventive in your approach.
- Find something that suits you, applying it in a way that is appropriate in your particular circumstances.

Habits of mind control our lives

Practices of this nature can bring immediate advantages, as is seen from the example given. They also confer long-term advantages, because it is our habit of mind more than the occasional brilliant idea which controls our lives.

Habits of mind generate the environment in which we live. Everything that involves us is filtered through them. Our habits of mind affect our understanding of events, and affect our response to them. New possibilities will naturally arise, as will new ways of dealing with perennial problems. By adopting a reflective habit of mind we give them permission to arise. Acknowledging in practice the presence of the Venus Principle is a habit to overcome habit, a way of freeing oneself from the habitual response, broadening the mind, climbing out of entrenched positions, creating new forms that perfectly meet the existing situation. Without doubt, if the match between need and response is perfect, success must be assured.

In this whole process of love, the first thing you have to learn to love is yourself. The deeper you enter your own inner being the easier this will become. The love you find within is no different from the love you find in the full relationship you have with the world around you and all that it holds. One reflects the other.

PRACTICE

• Practice the habit that overcomes habit. Have faith in yourself, and turn to the principle of love within. Do this over and over again.

Alert to the offer

If you are to find what it is that fully unlocks your potential in life, your way of serving life to the full, then you must consider what's on offer, those things that are asked of you. Serve those things to the uttermost. Say 'yes' in the spirit of dedication and devotion. You never know what is possible until you make the attempt. You never know what your contribution might be, what your own individual talents are, until you take up the offer. This offer may have been left lying on the table for a long time, totally unnoticed. Often the opportunity is lost through a lack of confidence, or by being too rigidly focused on something else, or simply not being alert enough to realize that an offer is actually being made.

And remember this is an offer being made to you personally. The energy that might be converted into deeds through you is universal, but the means is quite particular. You are the means. Listen to these words by Martha Graham, the dancer and choreographer, who made full use of the offers that came her way.

There is a vitality, a life force, an energy, a quickening that is translated through you into action, and because there is only one of you in all time, this expression is unique. And if you block it, it will never exist through any other medium and will be lost.

If you are unwilling to take up the offer because of personal doubts, deep misgivings about yourself or even a hint of self-loathing, then the chances of seeing those opportunities, let alone meeting them, are greatly reduced.

Equally forceful is the opposite. What's on offer may be considered beneath your dignity or something equally pompous. Whenever the promptings of the ego are heard, positive or negative, ignore them. While we are locked into such habitual modes of thought, a proper understanding of our opportunities is impossible. Leave all that. Turn to the situation in front of you. Open your heart and meet the need. If nothing comes to mind, or if you fail, forget self-recrimination, or fear of any sort. Negative emotion cuts you off from the situation and from yourself. No, you must look again.

This is important for you personally. More important still is that in denying your opportunity, the opportunity is lost for everybody. If you don't take up the offer, you can't make the offer. Everybody misses out.

PRACTICE

- Be alert to the offer.
- Be confident, not so much in yourself but in the energy that could flow through you if you gave it the opportunity to flow.
- Meet the situation with reason and emotion. Both have their roots in love

Pulling the plug

The supply comes to us artists from the source of everything, as you know, whenever an idea comes of itself on its own wings. This is the inexhaustible source and the same impetus which sends the idea brings with it the power of carrying it out, which implies nourishment, shelter, friends, peace of mind, everything. The only thing one has to do is not block up the channels through which the supply comes.

These are the words of the painter Winifred Nicholson. Here she is writing of the supply of inexhaustible energy that an artist may touch in a moment of power and insight. The only danger, as she so clearly indicates, is of something personal blocking the channels. But what is that 'something personal'? All those things we have been discussing and will continue to discuss: habits of mind and emotional constraints in all their multifarious forms. They wait in the wings, ready to rule, laying limitations on everything we meet. In the process these limitations make a heavy claim. They claim to be us, and we believe them. More fool us. Pull the plug. Let the energy flow. Be creative, be constructive, serve the need in the spirit of love.

I received an e-mail from a friend recently. She had been asked to take a major role in the retraining of the senior management of a leading company in the US. It is requests such as this that usually get these negative characters out in full force. This is how she tackles the task:

It is a privilege and an enormous challenge. I have found that courage is what happens when one doesn't have time for hesitation or doubt, and that love in the present moment is the thread. Courage and love bring forth the wisdom that is needed, thank God. It works every time.

Without doubt the reason why she got the job was because she has the capacity for responding like this.

PRACTICE

- Courage and love provide the means for responding positively.
- Pull out the plug of habit and enter the present. That is where the energy lives.

Conscious and habitual will

Everything we do is the result of will, but there is both mechanical and conscious will. Mechanical will is the automatic response to events. It arises out of habit, the way we have always done things. There is nothing new about it. Within our subtle set-up there are whole sets of conditioned responses to meet every situation, just so long as they are similar to things we have faced in the past. For this we must be very grateful. To learn every mechanical operation over and over again would be a tedious business, but to allow the mechanical operation of the mind to spread to every aspect of human endeavour would turn us into automatons. It would prevent any kind of advance being made, because every thought, every action would be referred to the past. Every situation, even the most mundane, must have something new about it. To treat the new as if it were old is no way to develop as a human being.

For there to be anything new brought to any situation, there must be recourse to consciousness. Conscious will is action arising out of real connection. Acknowledging the presence is a way of making that connection, of freeing ourselves from the automatic response. As we have been discussing, it is also a means of tapping that energy which empowers all things that are new, really new.

PRACTICE

- Meet events as if for the first time, because, no matter what habits of mind may suggest, it will be the first time.

The past is my past but the present is something else

What we must all remember is that, speaking personally, the past, by necessity, is my past, my collection of impressions, my set of emotions. Every event that we come across has its own integrity. If we try to draw each event into our own private set-up and deal with it in the way we always deal with things, we may encourage habit, we may feed the ideas we hold about ourselves, we may serve our cherished identifications, but we will do little for the event itself except to lay some kind of artificial claim upon it. To truly serve the situation, we may very well have to lay aside some of our most cherished possessions.

These possessions are very close in. They materialize in all the things we gather around us. They are the ideas we hold about ourselves and the world in general.

These ideas may have immense validity, but only in as much as they meet what is happening now. How can we go out and serve the current situation if all the time we are trying to draw events into our own private set-up? If we do take such a line, then the line we create becomes a hard and fast one that clearly divides our world from everybody else's. To try and meet any situation from such a divided state must clearly have its effect. By introducing the Venus Principle, the approach completely changes. Senses turn out; thoughts turn out. Our view enlarges and we embrace the whole.

PRACTICE

Ask yourself these questions:
- What am I trying to defend in creating these artificial barriers?
- How may I breach my own defence lines?

Letting things come to their proper fruition

Your work in the world can only be undertaken by one person – yourself. All of us have our part to play. Our work can be called a success only when in some way it serves our fellow man. This is a primary principle on the way of love.

This approach has been recommended in all traditions of wisdom for all time. Here, from India, the sage Swami Ramdas expresses this thought:

Just as a flower gives out its fragrance to whomsoever approaches or uses it, so love from within us radiates towards everybody and manifests as spontaneous service.

Now this thought may be dismissed as a pleasant if somewhat idealistic approach, but in the real world ... What is being presented here, however, is of immense practical value. Not only does it lift the burden of life, reduce the strain, bring back a sense of fun, but it provides a resource for new and profoundly creative ideas. It allows you to love life and create what is just right for the situation and is therefore of immense value; for example, new ways of conducting business, new ideas for products, new ways of teaching, new ways of meeting problems in the family, of making and mending relationships. There is no area of human experience that may not be affected by this approach.

What is most affected, of course, is ourselves. What is being suggested here is not so much a matter of introducing something from without, but touching something within, something that has been there all along but left undiscovered and ignored. To practically apply the Venus Principle is a way of touching life at a much greater depth, of discovering happiness and a proper way for our capabilities to come to full fruition.

This is of immediate practical value, so we must start the process of re-educating our minds. Education is derived from the Latin word *educare*, which means 'to draw out'. What we are seeking to draw out in this process of re-education is the principle of love, a principle that lies at the bottom of everything but is often buried, either by circumstance or the prevailing habit of mind. Our task is to discover in practice what has lain there all along, and to allow the fullness of love to inform every aspect of life. We are speaking of creativity. Only by acknowledging the presence of love may we create the things that perfectly meet the need. This is doing something for the love of it. Take this task on board as a practical proposition.

PRACTICE

- Do whatever it is that comes your way, out of love for Love. This is no heavy moral duty, but a light and playful thing. It's how to be genuinely creative. Once practised, any other approach will seem ridiculous.

Chapter two

Coming into harmony

T HIS BOOK IS DEVOTED to the principle of love. We have already seen how in considering the nature of love and allowing that consideration to be explored in the practice of living, there comes automatically a deeper appreciation of life's fullness and an ability to respond more creatively to what comes our way.

And why do we feel it necessary to consciously undertake something like this? Why doesn't it all come readily to hand? The great German poet Goethe was certain of the reason.

Man surrenders so easily to the commonplace, his mind and his senses are so easily blunted, shut so quickly to supreme beauty that we must do all that we can to keep the feeling for it alive. No one can do without beauty entirely; it is only because people have never learned to enjoy what is really good that they delight in what is flat and futile so long as it is new.

Our task must be to find delight in something beyond the commonplace, allow beauty in some form to touch us, for only in this way may we be granted insight into the true nature of love.

By attempting to penetrate the surface of human experience and by exploring the principles that live within our hearts, we may learn to listen to our inner knowledge. That knowledge possesses its own beauty.

Existing within us are common features which we all recognize, if but dimly, and even though these features are often ignored they periodically burst through and find their expression. Rather than waiting for events to force an awareness of them upon us, they need to be attended to and understood, in the confidence that, with greater understanding, there follows a more creative approach, and a deeper appreciation of all that life offers.

In addition we will be examining the possibility, in experience, that simply by remembering the existence of these powers we come under their influence, and of these powers none is more powerful than the spirit of love.

PRACTICE

- Keep the feeling for beauty alive. Seek it out in any way that suits your nature. Consciously recognize it, whether it be in the form of words or music, art or architecture, or those of nature. Don't try to seize it. Simply rest in its presence, even if merely momentarily.

Life is all-consuming

We have this idea of enjoying life to the full, of draining our cup, but often instead of consuming life we are consumed by life. Tension, stress and anxiety gnaw away at us. Even when things appear to be turning out well, it doesn't take long for the familiar trio to come trotting on. Life doesn't need to be like this. The following, given to me recently, is an observation about how these consuming forces may be opposed.

It was a clear blue November day, with the first frost of the winter, and I was heading out of London for a critical business meeting that I was to chair. I had had a good night's sleep. I felt in an excellent frame of mind, particularly as the day was so beautiful.

But having arrived at St Pancras Station, I discovered that all the trains were up the creek due to 'circumstances beyond our control'. This later I discovered to be the frost. I got the delayed 7:30 which left at 8:10, feeling lucky because my meeting wasn't until 10:00, and I had plenty of time.

The train broke down ten minutes into the journey: 'mechanical problems'. I began to feel stressed. 'Why did it have to happen on such a day, affecting such a critical meeting?' Observing the 8:00 a.m. main line train pass an hour later didn't help matters, nor did it help to see the slower but operational commuter trains regularly pass.

I phoned ahead to make certain that someone could take my place until I arrived. Although I did all that was needed, it didn't help: I was still in a state of extreme agitation and frustration. I knew that my state would affect the meeting and that made it worse.

The words came to mind: 'What's the point of getting wound up about something you cannot influence? What a waste of energy!'

At that moment I decided to let go of my anger and frustration. I remembered the beauty that I had seen earlier in the day and looked out of the window at the sky. Earlier it had been sunrise with pink clouds. Now it was clear blue. I felt quite in awe of it, how striking it was, the beauty of the sunlight.

At last the train got moving, and immediately I felt all my old emotions come churning to the surface. I consciously slowed my breathing and looked back to the immensity of that blue sky.

When I finally got there, I was only five minutes late. I thought of using my bad journey in a positive way. I thought it might help the meeting.

'Life has positives and negatives just like this project. I want you to say whatever is on your mind, but if you have a negative view consider how it may be turned to the positive.

'I'm going to start. On the negative side, I've had a terrible journey. It's taken me two hours to do a 20 minute journey. I was worried that I was going to be late, and I hate being late. But on the positive side, I didn't go and buy any cigarettes, and I noticed what a beautiful sky it is today.'

A couple of people took the opportunity offered and got things off their chest. We went on to have a very constructive meeting. People came up to me afterwards and congratulated me on how it had been handled.

A few days later I wrote a poem about that sky, the first poem I had written for eight years.

This is a very perceptive observation and so informative about the art of living. You will notice from this woman's account that beauty and an 'excellent frame of mind' are intimately connected. In the frame of mind she was in at the start of the day, she couldn't help but be susceptible to beauty. There is nothing here about the dark passage from bed to office. She was alive to possibility, excepting the possibility of the train being late. On this discovery, the possibilities closed down immediately. What happened to the open sky when she sat fuming on the train? It didn't go away, but for her it didn't exist. But even in this state she recognized the loss of energy, and that without this energy she would be incapable of dealing with the forthcoming meeting in an intelligent way.

When reason finally intervened, she rose above negative emotion and discovered the beauty of the sky once more. With the discovery of beauty, energy returned. This energy, when the train finally began to move, enabled her to keep from falling back into her former state of tension, stress and anxiety. Not only that, it suggested a new and creative way of opening the meeting, a way that perfectly met the situation.

To connect with this energy is the most important lesson in life, and it can only be done through love. What is this 'excellent frame of mind' she found herself in at the beginning of her day if not the principle of love working through her? When you feel good, how do you respond to others, to life in general? It is certainly not by withdrawing and cutting yourself off. It's certainly not by being debilitated by doubts and fears. And, in turn, doesn't the giving of yourself generate its own energy, enabling your to deal with difficult situations, allowing your mind to be open to new possibilities, disarming the negative and finding happiness? Under these circumstances, rather than being consumed by life, life feeds you and does what it is supposed to do: it provides vitality.

PRACTICE

Hold the following questions in mind:
- Am I eating or being eaten? If being eaten, by what am I being consumed?
- Where is the 'blue sky' to which I might turn, that might open my heart and mind?

Finding the harmony

The other noticeable feature of the story you have just read is the movement out of a separate state into one of harmony. Harmony expresses the underlying unity in things that appear to be separate. Sometimes the underlying unity has to be consciously recognized, deliberately attended to if there is any chance of harmony arising.

Reason will readily confirm that unity cannot be experienced from a state of separation. In the example, beauty was the key – it freed the woman from a state of growing frustration. Beauty cannot be recognized without there being an opening to its possibility, first an opening of the senses and then of the heart and mind.

In this state the great divide between 'me and the rest' – which can so easily dominate our way of viewing the world – gives way to an intuitive knowledge of the underlying unity. This underlying unity, rather than being something devoid of any feature, is in fact a great sea of possibility, the very source of the energy that provides all kinds of new opportunities and, additionally, a more profound understanding of what already exists.

Despite a century where so much of art has been devoted to discord, our current understanding of this word 'harmony' still retains the sense of parts in the context of the whole. The *Oxford English Dictionary* defines harmony as arising out of a relationship of parts in order to create a consistent or orderly whole, and following on from this a feeling of peaceableness and concord.

The great pleasure to be found in anything properly composed is the awareness both of the elements of the composition and the unity out of which the whole thing is arising. That unity is conveyed by the sense of satisfaction the work provides.

In his famous book on architectural principles, *De re aedificatoria*, the great Renaissance figure Leon Battista Alberti, writes of beauty and harmony

I shall define beauty to be a harmony of all the parts, in whatsoever subject it appears, fitted together with such proportion and connection, that nothing could be added, diminished or altered, but for the worse.

This kind of beauty and harmony can only arise when the principle of unity is held in mind and known by heart throughout the composition of the work.

PRACTICE

- When taking on any task, avoid getting locked into the detail. Be aware instead of how the detail not only serves the whole but arises out of it.
- Step back and connect with the bigger picture, not by trying to grasp everything all at once, but by simply acknowledging that part must be part of the whole.

Limitless possibility

I was speaking to a friend the other day about music. He is a teacher, and he was telling me about something he often tells his students: that music arises moment by moment, that the composition is not to be found at the end of the piece, but only in the notes that are being played at that moment.

That's where the real substance is to be found. You don't get any prizes for getting to the end of the piece but only by connecting with the beauty that arises as you play.

We are often in life subject to a linear way of thinking, believing that a thing has worth only in its completion, and it is to that end we strive. But only in the moment might we discover the underlying sea of creativity out of which the whole thing is arising. We must teach the mind that real completion is to do with a movement on the vertical axis, diving deep rather than simply scurrying along the horizontal plane, desperate to achieve some kind of preconceived idea of getting to the end.

By diving deep, the end is looked after by what is known in the moment, moment by moment.

Remember what Mozart, that great master of creativity, said about composition? He referred to the quiet joy that follows from it, of how in a good state of mind the ideas flowed as if from nowhere and formed themselves into a beautiful composition that could be heard not as successive movements but all in a moment.

Mozart was a man who lived on intimate terms with harmony, who knew from experience the joy of the parts standing in the presence of the whole. When people speak of 'the depth, the vast extent of his musical genius', what is this 'depth' and 'extent' if nothing more than the expression of a vast underlying sea of creativity out of which the whole thing is arising?

PRACTICE

- When faced by any task, great or small, not only be aware of the method, the system, the desired objective, but also of the moment of manifestation as it arises out of limitless possibility.
- Enjoy the music of manifestation rather than trying to force events to some kind of preconceived conclusion. By attacking things in this way you can only work from separation, forcing things to comply with your will and following from it the inevitable satisfaction at success or frustration at failure.
- Always strive to work from unity, creatively accepting what is offered in the moment, playing your part at the point of manifestation, loving it by being there, gaining all the energy you need to meet the situation from that love.

Work like a lover

Parts remain as parts until we see the whole. We can begin to see the whole when we start making connections. Any connection is a step out of separation. With the connection comes the energy.

One of the great architects of the 20th century, Le Corbusier, expressed this desire:

I would like architects – not just students – to pick up a pencil and draw a plant, a leaf, the spirit of a tree, the harmony of a sea shell, formations of clouds, the complex play of waves spreading out on a beach, so as to

*discover different expressions of an inner force. I would like their hands and
minds to become passionately involved in this kind of intimate investigation.*

*We say a face is beautiful when the precision of its modelling and the
disposition of its features reveal proportions we find harmonious – harmonious because deep down, beyond the range of our senses, they produce a
resonance, a sort of sounding board that begins to vibrate: a sign of some
indefinable absolute operating in the depths of our being.*

What is this resonance of which he speaks? Resonance occurs
when something starts to vibrate in harmony with something else.
We talk about something striking a chord. On such occasions an
inner knowledge is aroused. It may accord with something that has
already been experienced in our lives, or something that is deeply
inherent within all of us regardless of our experience, that has been
there from the beginning. It is this that Le Corbusier calls an 'indefinable absolute'. This 'indefinible absolute' is aroused by the 'intimate investigation' he speaks of. Out of that intimacy arises a
depth of knowledge both of the thing itself under investigation
and of something deep within ourselves.

PRACTICE

- Work like a lover. Give of yourself passionately to the work in
  hand. Take pleasure in even the simplest things: touch, taste,
  smell, sight, listening. Enjoy the intimate connection that arises
  out of the present moment.

Finding a cure for boiled brains

When we connect with the harmony to be discovered in great
music or great architecture, a recognition of the same principle of
harmony that lies dormant within our souls is awakened. Like the
recognition of beauty, we would not be able to recognize such
harmonies if it were not for the harmonies within. Outer beauty
and outer harmony awaken the soul to the consciousness of
harmony and beauty within. These are the unheard melodies
which Keats assures us are sweeter than those that are heard.

In the final act of *The Tempest*, the great magician Prospero summons up heavenly music as the final part of his creative cure for psychological disorder. He calls 'solemn airs' the 'best comforters to unsettled fancies'. He fully recognizes how they can cure our brains, 'now useless and boiled within our skulls.'

Speaking from our own experience, what is it that boils our brains? We talk about first fuming and then boiling over with rage. Very often this rage arises out of frustration. We simply can't lay our hands on what we desire. This is certainly the case with the people Prospero is treating. Their whole lives are devoted to the attainment of personal desire, and by as much as they obtained those desires so they lost themselves. In restoring them to harmony, he allows them to come to a state of self-knowledge. In the process the principles of justice and love inevitably find their full and proper manifestation. In the simple terms that we have been exploring, they move out of a state of separation into one of unity.

There is no doubt that surrounding ourselves with things that are by nature harmonious has an effect on body and mind. Beauty heals and so does harmony. The philosophers of old were certain that the harmonies we hear with the ears and see with the eyes may suggest those immortal harmonies that all of us hold in our hearts if we could but connect with them. We must consciously expose ourselves to things harmonic, train our minds to think harmoniously and come to recognize the healing power of harmony. Harmony has the power to pacify even the most discordant elements of mind and body, and in the process, like Prospero's patients, bring us to a state of self knowledge.

When talking about the difference between architecture and engineering, Le Corbusier expressed this opinion:

The purpose of engineering is to create structures. The purpose of architecture is to create emotions. Architectural emotion arises when a work strikes a chord within us that harmonizes with universal laws we recognize, submit to and admire. When certain proportions are established, the work takes hold of us. Architecture is proportion – a creation of the mind.

PRACTICE

Seek out the principle of harmony. Surround yourself with things that are harmonious. Clear the clutter from your home, from your work place, in order that what remains may be recognized as being in harmony, everything having its purpose, and effect. What goes for one's outer circumstances also applies to the inner. In fact the two are in no way separate. Clear the inner clutter. By consciously recognizing the principle of harmony in all things, we will inevitably clear the decks. In the process the energy which is devoted to sustaining the useless clutter – which usually does nothing but dull the mind and create confusion – will be devoted to more positive ends, ends which by their very nature are creative and harmonious.

Grateful for the hammering

The following are words by the great Renaissance philosopher, Marsilio Ficino. They are, of course, very much in accord with what we have been discussing, as they concern harmony and love.

Light, gracefulness, proportion, number and measure which we apprehend by thought, vision, hearing, it is towards these that the ardour of the genuine lover strives.

Rather than considering these words directly, let's instead return to our architectural theme, not by further pondering on the grand conceptions of Alberti or Le Corbusier but by considering a story concerning much more humdrum matters.

It's another of those observations which the people attending the classes I take love to relate and which I love to hear, because it is so informative of the right way to live and so confirmative of the principles we discuss in these groups. The woman speaking is an architect and comes from New Zealand. She is by nature mild and not particularly assertive. She does, however, know the practical aspects of her job and is quite used to wading across building sites, intent on ensuring that what she has designed is properly constructed.

In New Zealand we are very used to timber-framed housing. In England it is not so common. Even carpenters often use wood like bricks. I have recently been working on the second phase of this residential development which uses timber-framed construction methods.

When I first went on site all I could hear was this furious banging. There were all these builders intent on demonstrating their strength, hammering these frames together, but it was all being done badly. There is a procedure to these things of which they were unaware. Because of this the work they were producing was simply not accurate enough.

Having seen this I insisted that they took apart what they had done and start again. This did not please them. To be told to do this would have angered them at the best of times, but to be told by a woman how to nail wooden frames together – by tradition, a man's preserve – was not something easily accepted, especially when I was still not satisfied after their second attempt. I showed them again, and all the time I felt this mounting barrage of anger, but they didn't understand the principle, and it was only when that understanding began to dawn could they see the point of my insistence. Finally they returned to work and gradually a far greater economy of effort began to arise. They became aware of the measure of the job, and all that masculine aggression began to fade.

The next time I came on site I heard a sound of hammering which was of an entirely different nature. The frames were being fixed with just the required amount of force and nothing more. There was such a sweetness about that sound.

Some of the work was going on above existing housing. I wondered how the people underneath survived. I spoke to one young mother. She said that, rather than objecting, she was grateful for the hammering, as it lulled her baby off to sleep. She thought she might make a recording to use after the men had finished.

Needless to say that after they had mastered the techniques involved, these men took great pleasure and pride in their work.

Perhaps, after all, this story has everything to do with grace, proportion, lightness, thought and vision. These are all expressions of beauty and harmony and their inevitable product, for what did the men's pride and pleasure arise from but the love of what they were doing and the fulfilment that comes from a job well done?

The qualities of lightness of touch, economy of action, grace and vision are certainly present here, as is courage. It certainly called for a degree of courage to take on all that male aggression, to quietly insist that the work should proceed properly, and then to demonstrate and then insist that the builders do it again and then again. That takes courage. It also demonstrates an adherence to what she knew to be true. It is so easy to be deflected in the face of adversity, and ignore that which we know to be true. You could imagine the difference in that building if she hadn't insisted. There would have been one distraught mother to begin with.

PRACTICE

- Remember the principles of harmony, proportion and measure, and then work with economy, saying and doing nothing unnecessary. When faced with adversity this may take courage, but be grateful for the hammering. Strength may come from adversity.
- Be determined to stay true, remembering that the most convincing discouragement arises within. Ignore the voice that says give up.

But who is Harmony?

Another point made by Ficino is:

The harmony we make with musical instruments and voices is the image of divine Harmony.

Given that we are exploring the nature of harmony it would be useful to discover who exactly Harmony is and what exactly is her nature.

In Greek mythology Harmonia is the daughter of Mars and Venus, respectively the god of war and the goddess of love.

Harmony stands therefore as a mean between the two, both the cause and the result of a loving agreement. According to this way of thinking, harmony tempers extremes. Is harmony then merely some universal middle ground, neither one thing nor the other?

In mathematics the mean is the binding of two extremes by a single term. Plato claims that it is by a study of the mean that one can approach an understanding of the laws that govern creation.

The mean not only allows for the expansion of number and form but also allows an inner recognition of and return to the underlying unity from which all number arises.

Some have said that love is the ultimate mean. Within the field of love all forms rise and are known, both the physical forms detected by the senses, and also the subtle forms of thought and emotion. It is through the recognition of the unity that lies behind and gives rise to the great diversity of things that conflicting forms may be drawn into something which is entirely concordant and harmonious.

By its very nature love is to be found beneath the surface aspect of all forms, waiting to be tapped.

This is what Frank Lloyd Wright, the great American architect, has to say about the function of the creative artist:

This is what it means to be an artist – to seize this essence brooding every-where, just behind aspect.

What traditional wisdom constantly tells us is that the more profound the recognition of this essence, the more we appreciate harmony. The more we appreciate harmony, the more we are able to express harmony in our thoughts and deeds.

Ficino, speaking from his classical background, called this realm Jove, as did the other philosophers of the Platonic tradition:

Poetry arises from the Muses and the Muses from Jove. The followers of Plato repeatedly call the soul of the whole universe Jove, who inwardly nourishes heaven and earth, the moving seas, the moon's shining orb, the stars and sun. Permeating every limb, he moves the whole mass and mingles with its vast substance.

Shakespeare calls Jove the Tenth Muse. He was, after all, father of the muses, Mnemosyne (Memory) being their mother. Shakespeare dismisses the other nine, and goes instead straight to source for his inspiration:

> *How can my muse want subject to invent*
> *While thou dost breathe, that por'st into my verse*
> *Thine own sweet argument, too excellent*
> *For every vulgar paper to rehearse?*
> *O, give thanks, if aught in me*
> *Worthy perusal stand against thy sight;*
> *For who's so dumb that cannot write to thee,*
> *When thou thyself dost give invention light?*
> *Be thou the tenth Muse, ten times more in worth*
> *Than those old nine which rhymers invocate,*
> *And he that calls on thee, let him bring forth*
> *Eternal numbers to outlive long date.*
> *If my slight muse do please these curious days,*
> *The pain be mine, but thine shall be the praise.*

We are now really in the realm of poetry and poetic invention. But why not?

PRACTICE

- Read these quotations again slowly to yourself. They have their own power. Remember how, according to Shakespeare, the poet's words make even the gods grow drowsy with the harmony.
- Plato says that harmonious forms are 'meant to correct any discord which may have arisen in the courses of the soul, and to be our ally in bringing her into harmony and agreement with herself'.

    Read the quotations with this thought in mind, slowly and reflectively.

By what are we fed?

What effect do Shakespeare's words have on you? I remember that one day, out of the blue, my father brought home the complete works of Shakespeare. I was about six or seven at the time. I always meant to ask him why he had done this, but never did. People speak of powerful influences coming to bear upon their lives. This was one such influence on mine. He read from one of these books. I didn't understand a word, but I did know that these words were of supreme importance. It was if I knew them already even though their significance was obscure.

This is an example of Menemosyne (memory) in operation. It arouses that which has always been there, but needs to be awoken. When this kind of memory is called forth then the soul, to quote Socrates, is 'brought into agreement and harmony with herself'.

Now read these lines from the great Persian poet, Rumi:

> 'Tis said, the pipe and lute that charms our ears
> Derive their melody from rolling spheres...
>
> We, who are parts of Adam, heard with him
> The song of angels and seraphim.
> Our memory, though dull and sad, retains
> Some echo still of unearthly strains.
> Oh, music is the meat of all who love,
> Music uplifts the soul to realms above.
> The ashes glow, the latent fires increase;
> We listen and are fed with joy and peace.

By turning to the expression of harmony in the form of the words we read or the music we listen to, or in appreciating the beauty in the architectural forms that fill our towns and cities or by simply creating an harmonious environment in which to live, we are evoking the principle of Harmony. She has her beauty, and once we have made a full connection with that beauty, then the power of love cannot help but be present.

At the beginning of this chapter I quoted Goethe. Here is part of that quotation again:

Man surrenders so easily to the commonplace, his mind and his senses are so easily blunted, shut so quickly to supreme beauty that we must do all that we can to keep the feeling for it alive.

PRACTICE

- Enjoy things well expressed. There's poetry to be found everywhere. Listen to music with respect. Even great music can be turned into 'muzak' when no proper connection is made. Listen with both ears.
- Be conscious of composition. Be aware of it everywhere. Learn to love harmony, however it might manifest. The mind can be so easily blunted. The melody is there but the instrument needs to be tuned.

Chapter three

Conquer fear through love

Fear and all its offshoots have a great hold on the modern mind. Stress and anxiety are the ones that receive most attention. Fear though takes many other forms and these accompany the streak of cynicism that gives our times its negative aspects: unease, despondency, mistrust and downright pessimism.

The things that we are fearful of are legion, many only dimly recognized, existing as some nagging anxiety sitting at the back of the mind, corroding our experience of life. Other fears may demand our attention more forcefully, but they have the same effect, isolating us within ourselves and cutting us off. We fear whatever threatens the things we hold dear. When we are in its grip, inevitably it colours our view of everything.

There is, however, a way of escaping these fears. Recently I was told this story. It was given as a dramatic illustration of how love might overcome fear.

The woman who told the story had been climbing in the Cairngorm mountains in Scotland with two friends, and night had fallen.

It was pitch black; there was thick snow and gale force winds. A continuous flow of falling snow made visibility almost nil and progress frighteningly slow.

I had been out in these conditions all day, but the excitement of the climb had made me unaware of increasing fatigue and freezing temperatures. After nine hours on the go, even reaching the top didn't prevent my spirits from falling.

Cautiously we started our two-hour trek off the mountain.

The dark meant our progress had to be slow. The situation was extremely dangerous, but by now I was just too tired to care.

I found myself contemplating stopping for a rest; I didn't feel able to go on, but I also knew that stopping could be fatal in such extreme conditions. My desire to give in frightened me, yet I was convinced I couldn't manage the arduous walk through waist-high snow drifts.

In desperation I turned away from my fears to connect with everything around me. Under these circumstances, it was actually easy to concentrate on what I could see of the scenery, the sound of the wind howling, the gleam of our torches on the snow, the sensation of freezing skin and layers of clothes, the weight of heavy boots and rucksack.

Minutes later I became aware that my pace had become steady, my breathing more regular, and I began to take pleasure in the very thing that minutes earlier had terrified me. I seemed to have tapped into reserves of energy I had been convinced were not there.

My increase of morale seemed to spread to the rest of the flagging group.

When we finally got to the bottom, not only did we find satisfaction at having survived the dangers we had endured, there was also a keen sense of the beauty discovered on the way.

This is a vivid example of an aspect of the law of love in operation. It may be formulated like this:

In as much as anxiety comes to dominate our emotional life so the power of love declines.

In as much as love dominates, so fear recedes.

In her story, the woman's overriding fear for her own safety is an obvious and understandable feature, but there was another fear, a fear that you would think would preserve life: the fear of giving up. But both these fears affected her in the same way; they made her draw back into herself, separating her from all that surrounded her, leaching away her energy, the very thing she needed most.

Consider carefully what transformed the situation.

She turned outwards, she made connection with the world around her. She withdrew her mind from the source of her debilitation – her fear. Instead, she made connection with the beauty of her surroundings.

When fear dominates the mind, everything becomes drab, but when beauty rises, and we make conscious connection, the love that was there unseen springs immediately into life. And notice how it can be so easily communicated. When her spirits rose, everybody was affected. They all found new energy.

Love and beauty are intimately connected. By necessity we find great beauty in the things we love., and from that love we gain strength.

My daughter recently gave birth. My wife was her birth partner. She wanted her mother. She did brilliantly, but there were moments of fear in which she turned to her mother for comfort and strength. Afterwards she expressed it all in these simple words: 'I loved the smell of your shirt.'

PRACTICE

- When fear dominates the mind, turn your attention out, away from the internal nagging.
- Connect with the beauty that is always there, whether it be through sight, through hearing, through touch or taste. If the fear returns, reconnect with the beauty.

Slip out of separation

When most of us experience fear it is not in some life-threatening situation where fear may very well have a part to play. It's much more subtle and insidious. It takes the form of background anxiety.

When fear takes a real hold we become completely buried by regrets for the past and worries for the future, thoughts and feelings which enclose and separate. Both are a rich source for anger. This chain of emotion reduces the consciousness available to us. As for the universal principles which we discussed in the last chapter, with a reduction of consciousness we are even more emphatically separated from the likes of Mercury and Venus: Reason and Love. Instead, we live alone surrounded by all the things we have identified with in the past. Out of fear, we jealously protect these possessions. We are proud of some of them, about others we feel considerable guilt. In them all we have invested our identity, and the greatest fear for us as individuals is losing that possession with which we feel most identified, ourselves.

On the other hand, love by necessity conjoins, draws together, throws down barriers and encourages. It allows us as individuals to make contact with the universal. Under the influence of love, the heart is opened and the experience of life is transformed. With this transformation, there naturally arises a deeper connection with the world around us and with that comes a sense of inner freedom. We are freed from separation, petty concern, habitual patterns of thought, obstacles that hold us within a framework of self-imposed limitations which we, acting as individuals, must inevitably be subject to. When these patterns of thought and emotion hold sway, our experience of life is totally formed by them. There is no other recourse available to us.

Only the principle of love allows us to look beyond the impediments that the enclosed condition forces upon us. Enclosed by our minds and bodies and the desires and aversions which they sustain, we find it difficult to love and be loved.

The philosophers of old believed that the single most effective cure for fear was to be found in the service of love.

PRACTICE
• When you are locked into a cycle of fear and regret, see what the current situation demands and serve that.

In giving we receive

How many times have we found that in giving we receive? How many times have we felt that we are not up to facing more demands?

When this thought is uppermost, the tiredness increases. But, no sooner do we go out to meet a need that has arisen, the tiredness disappears and we wonder where the energy has come from.

As a teacher I have experienced this over and over again. The students' needs wipe out self consideration. This is not at all an unusual experience. All of us must have experienced something of the same, for it happens everywhere – at home, at work, when dealing with problems and concerns, in all aspects of human experience. Although it's not at all unusual, it is good to recognize it for what it is. It is not just by chance that this happens. It is the principle of love working in us all. It's that which supplies the energy.

Notice how in the story at the start of this chapter the woman discovered something, an essential principle. By as much as she turned outwards, so she found a resource within. In giving she received. The same applies to all of us. By as much as we overcome our confining thoughts, so the strength is there. In her situation she found beauty instead of fear, and inner strength in the face of extreme danger.

This is a major discovery on the path of love.

By giving we receive.

By as much as we overcome confining thought, so we discover our own inner source of energy.

Because it forms part of everybody's personal experience, such occurrences can be easily overlooked, but we should be encouraged to take note of them and having recognized them, consciously apply them. It's good to be thoughtful and then act on what we discover.

PRACTICE

- Apply the principle: in giving we receive. Test it in experience and note the result.

Cracking the nut

Our states of mind confine more than any outer circumstances. In Shakespeare's *Hamlet*, Hamlet himself makes this interesting statement:

I could be bounded in a nutshell and count myself king of infinite space were it not that I have bad dreams.

When you consider how small the confines of a nut are and how vast space is, you might think that he is somewhat labouring a point. The point he is making, however, in his vivid way, is that subtle forces of the mind confine far more than any physical imprisonment. He felt he would be free even if he were shut up in a nutshell, except for one thing: 'bad dreams'. Anybody who has seen the play will know what his 'bad dreams' are, but what are ours? The dreaming state is generally thought to be confined to sleep, but it extends to our waking hours. What are the waking dreams that limit our thinking?

Very often these limitations are caused by our private fears, fears that the things we hold dear may be taken from us: our money, our pleasures, our jobs, our status, our health, our happiness, the good opinion of others, our pride. We fear that the beliefs we hold may be proved wrong, or that somehow we may be exposed as being a little less than we pretend to be. We are fearful that what goes towards making us believe we are somebody may somehow be taken from us. Such fearfulness has the power to create anxiety and, following on from that, ill health. The time, and hence money, lost to industry through stress-related illness is proof of how pervasive fear is. When fear can be measured in terms of the balance sheet, there arises a strong desire to measure the pervasivness of fear.

The irony is that the very thing that we are fearful of, the loss of health, happiness and peace of mind, is encouraged by fear itself.

But love conquers fear. Our fears would be diminished if we found ways of serving and expressing love, because our thoughts would be devoted to the things we love and not be confined by fears about ourselves.

PRACTICE

- Look outwards, turn outwards.
- Meet the need that is presenting itself now.
- Recognize the beauty in that need.

No fear in the present

I was taking a discussion group recently when such matters were under consideration, and one of the group members made an observation. He is a paramedic, a man used to dealing with emergencies. His working life is devoted to the service of others, but he too has his personal problems.

I was called out on an emergency. A man had climbed up some scaffolding which was cladding an office block and was threatening to jump off. I was called upon to go up and persuade him to come down. These things do happen, but I have this problem. I suffer from vertigo. I can't even look at a photograph taken from the top of a cliff or a tall building without feeling the effects.

But suddenly, there I was, making my way up this scaffolding, hand over hand. I was vividly aware of the whole thing: the hardness of the steel under my hands, the space around me. I knew exactly what to do. The whole thing was so clear, and I had all the time in the world. When I got to the top, again I knew exactly what to do, how to approach him, what words to say, and remarkably there was not one moment of fear throughout.

When reading this story, you might like to consider these points:
- To whom or what were his actions devoted?
- Where was his attention?
- What effect did this have upon his habitual fear?

What is evident is that although the action in general was devoted to saving the other man's life, the attention of the paramedic was at every point centred on what was immediately to hand, literally. He had an overall intention, but where the attention was resting, moment by moment, was on what was happening in that moment. Ever played tennis? The game is won by being there, shot by shot, not by picturing yourself celebrating winning when the game ends.

To return to the first question about the dedication of the action, it is worth noting that the picture the paramedic held of himself as a man who hated heights didn't play any part in the event, nor were there any other personal considerations, of being a hero for instance.

You might say that he was merely doing his job. As a paramedic he is called on to meet all kinds of emergencies. There is no doubt that in doing his job he has to play his part to the full. And that is exactly the point; working like this is called dedication.

Strikingly, there is nothing here about what he could or he couldn't do, what he was prepared to do and what he wasn't prepared to do. Self-imposed limitations had nothing to do with it. He made the observation to illustrate the dropping away of limitations. And the limitations went, simply because the need was all.

Later on in the conversation he returned to the story and added a telling reflection. He said that in addition to his sense impressions being heightened during the drama, there were two other factors. One was knowledge. He knew exactly where to place his hands and feet. He knew exactly how to approach the man, both physically and mentally. The other factor was, of course, the lack of fear. He concluded by saying:

Strangely enough, in the present there appears to be no fear. Fear belongs to the past and the future.

Fear may be the direct cause of action, but in the midst of it all, when you are really in the present, there is no fear. Fear is about projecting the past into the future.

REFLECTION

- Reflect upon this man's observation.
- The next time you feel afflicted by anxiety and stress, leave the past and future and return to the immediate need.

The foundation of morality

There is a well known philosophical paper delivered by Schopenhauer, the 19th century German philosopher, called *The Foundation of Morality*. In it he poses the question: 'How is it that a person can so participate in the perils of another that they are prepared to risk death in their service when self preservation is considered to be the first law of nature?'

At moments like this, Schopenhauer claimed, there is a metaphysical realization that you and the other person are one, and the sense of separation is only the effect of time and space. Our true reality is discovered in the unity of all life.

If this is true, he argued, all heroic action is a considered or spontaneous devotion to the realization of this truth.

Understandably, not many of us would stand up to be counted amongst the heroes. But Schopenhauer stated that when anyone serves the unity of the family, the unity of the nation, the unity of all mankind, or the unity of life itself, this may be considered an heroic act. In the small acts of service as in the large, the hero is found. That was Schopenhauer's belief.

This same belief has been formulated in various ways throughout the history of recorded thought. It is indeed present whenever there is a rise in the state of consciousness. It is the acknowledgment of the Principle of Love in operation.

By this argument, merely reading this book and attempting to put something of what is to be discovered in these pages into practice could be described as an heroic act, for what are we doing reading a book about the nature of love but serving that unity? Are we not, in essence, trying to free ourselves from the narrow perspective, widen our vision, connect in some way to the greater whole?

According to all the great systems of philosophy, when one frees oneself from the effects of 'me and mine' then bliss is found. Even a small step in this direction, a small act of love, a deed done in memory of the life that unites us all, is a deed done in the service of humanity, for the self of all mankind.

This is indeed loving thy neighbour as thyself. No one is left out, including yourself. It doesn't act like a command. It works of necessity.

Schopenhauer used weighty terms like 'the foundation of morality' but this foundation is all very playful.

We have a baby in the house. To see him playfully kicking his legs in the air is a joy. It may not seem like the stuff of sacrifice or obligation – not in the way we normally think of sacrifice and obligation. Nor may it seem to make any great intellectual demand. And you may not be able to get ahead seeing a baby kick his legs – not in the way we normally think of getting ahead – but that is rather missing the point. The play is everything. With love on one side and love on the other, what else can there be but love in the middle? So easily we become bound to the treadmill of doing and achieving, chained twice over by the fear of failure. But with love …

Shantananda Saraswati, one of the great sages of modern India, spoke these simple words.

This play is due to love … There is nothing besides love. This is the real work. Here people are only instruments and the creation is bliss. If one could establish the same relationship in daily work, then the doer would be the instrument and the receiver would also be an instrument and the two would become One. The unity thus achieved would become a fountain of happiness.

PRACTICE

- When you find yourself in the midst of desperate concern, treat the whole thing as a play.
- Be a hero, certainly, but do it playfully.
- With love there is always a full response but with a light touch.

Our life is shaped by our mind

In the *Dhammapada* the Buddha writes:

Our life is shaped by our mind; we become what we think. Suffering follows an evil thought as the wheels of a cart follow the oxen that draw it.

Our life is shaped by our mind; we become what we think. Joy follows a pure thought like a shadow that never leaves.

Whatever we dwell on must have its effects on our understanding and impression of life. We are shaped by these thoughts just as much as we are by our genetic make up. In an age when determinism has met materialism, it is easy to become locked into a frame of mind that makes the possibility of change a slim one. According to the Buddha, we become what possesses the mind. If we constantly dwell on our fears, then by necessity we become fearful, and so full of fear that nothing else can force an entry.

Our life is shaped by our mind, and our mind is shaped by what it feeds on. Fear brings its own suffering, but where there is love everything is transformed.

When we look through history, it is noticeable how different a nation's fortunes are at different times. At one point nothing seems impossible, at another there is self-doubt and loss of vision. Have the people of that nation changed physically or has some kind of subtle transformation taken place? The Buddha was in no doubt: 'Our life is shaped by our mind.'

If we believe that we are nothing but our bodies then we may very well believe that all we amount to is forged by our genetic make-up. But we are not what our genes are. We are what we think, and certainly what we think may cause this beautiful physical set-up we all possess to malfunction. Why else is so much money lost in stress-related illness? This is proof surely of the way the physical is ruled by the subtle.

Trying to improve things by chemical intervention may have validity, but we should also recognize that it is a great error to deal merely with the effects of illness without tackling the underlying cause.

Disease means simply lack of ease. Fear is one of the major health concerns of our times in that major illnesses often follow in its train. Where there is not a physical manifestation, fear operates on a subtle level. We may go to great lengths to try to smother its presence, and many of the methods we choose may of themselves be destructive, but there is only one way to overcome fear: through love.

We certainly need to attend to the physical, in all ways, but we should never forget the underlying cause.

Our life is shaped by our mind; we become what we think. Joy follows a pure thought like a shadow that never leaves.

But when we do think about our life, we tend to think about something that stretches back into the past and on into the future. Shaping it may appear a difficult undertaking when thought of in this way. The opportunity to shape our lives is only presented at one time: now. The way we meet this present moment governs everything. Everything is transformed by meeting it with love rather than fear.

PRACTICE
- Stop to consider how you are shaping your life.
- What is it that is making a difference now?

Everyone's a miracle

Love seeketh not itself to please,
Nor for itself hath any care,
But for another gives its ease,
And builds a heaven in hell's despair.

WILLIAM BLAKE

The impression of me and another is a wonderful starting point for any love affair. Obviously. What other alternative could there be? Narcissus may well have fallen in love with his own image reflected in the water, but, in the normal run of events, it's the thing opposite that forms the object of our devotion.

When the object of devotion is devotedly served, self-consideration is not uppermost in the mind. There is nothing like devoting yourself to something in order to get your mind off your own concerns. As I write my daughter is in the next room cooing over her baby. 'He's a gorgeous little person!' There's nothing there about her own situation. Nothing else is in her mind but the object of her devotion. Of everything else she is careless. The future has no appeal. The past does not exist. Everything is swallowed up in her immediate love. Under such blessed circumstances as the miracle of birth, love is utterly spontaneous. You don't have to deliberate. You don't have to construct anything. It's immediate. She gaily regales us with the impact her baby has had on her friends. All are drawn into her baby's presence. If anybody has any doubt about divine forces, be around at birth.

The same was true when my daughter was born. She was delivered at home. The midwife was well past retiring age, but somehow she stayed on, cycling out in the middle of the night. Miss Church was a local legend. Three generations had been drawn into the world by her hands. 'And everyone is a miracle.' That was her claim. And I have no reason to disbelieve her.

Sophocles, the great Greek tragedian, made this observation:

One word frees us from the weight and pain of life, and that word is love.

PRACTICE

- When bowed by your own concerns, meet the needs of others with the same mix of practicality and devotion that was so noticeable in a midwife who, even in her seventies, was prepared to cycle off in the middle of the night to deliver babies.

• When you have delivered others of their concerns, use the same means in delivering yourself of your own.

Free love

The two things that inevitably accompany pregnancy and child-birth are weight and pain. This is an outside observation, you understand, but my wife and daughter attest to it. The other thing that is evidently present, and this I can confirm, is love.

The essence of the Vedic concept of Dharma, the law for us all, is love. To put the concerns of others before our own concerns is the law of love. To see how it operates, notice how the more we become self-absorbed, the greater our insecurity becomes. If we are not unduly concerned about how we figure in the equation, there is little to be insecure about. There is certainly no doubt that we have a far greater chance of happiness if we make our object in life the care of others.

The cynic may claim that we are merely serving our own ends in serving others. 'You are only doing it because it makes you feel good.' The answer is, 'Of course!' Love is a universal principle. We may like to lay claim to it, but only because we like to lay claim to everything. Love, though, lies outside the personal, and when we serve Venus it frees us from the impediments that prevent the expression of love.

Love, therefore, is discovered just as much in those that give love as those that receive it. Have you ever tried to give love and not receive it? It's simply out of the question. The opposite equally applies. In trying to express anger you receive anger. In harming others you harm yourself. It certainly is in our own self-interest to avoid that. Serve instead the principle of love. It is natural for us to do so. Why do anything else?

When fear arises, when anger arises, when criticism arises, recognize them for what they are: impediments to that which is utterly natural to us all, the free expression of love. 'Building heaven in hell's despair' is not a matter of doing anything. It is merely a matter of refusing to submit to impediments that isolate us from our own essential nature.

Are we still talking about me and another or has something else arisen that links the apparent two, the unifying factor, love?

PRACTICE

- When the impediments to love appear, refuse to submit.
- When fear, in particular, comes to possess us, free love.

The power of words

To free love we must transcend limits. When love is held within limits then the attachments arise. We like to cling on to the things we are attached to, and in clinging on we fear to lose. Love and fear are intimately connected. When we are bound within circles of attachment, we like to control and manipulate the situation in order to serve our personal agenda. When we fear being thwarted in our intentions, anger rises in response. This is the stuff of office politics. It's the stuff of any power play. It might be quite fun at times, as long as we don't take it too seriously and don't mind losing. The problem is that we all too quickly get sucked in, even when we pretend we are not that concerned. Some of us don't even like losing at board games, let alone 'for real'. And what do people take 'for real'? Usually things like property, position, wealth and power.

In the *Cratylus*, Socrates talks about Pan, the double-formed son of Hermes. Pan represents speech. According to Socrates the smooth upper part indicates Pan's sacred form, which dwells with the gods above, whilst the lower part is rough like the goat of tragedy – 'for tales of falsehood have generally to do with the tragic or goatish life.' The problem is that when our involvements really take a grip, we fall foul of fear, anger, hate and deceit, the very substance of tragedy; not only tragedy, for farce also is made of much the same sort of stuff. Sophocles, as we have heard, has a simple response to such negative emotions and deceitful actions: love, but love of a certain kind.

When love works within confined limits there must be an inevitable lack of freedom. It's all about clinging on and fearing to lose. Room for manoeuvre is limited when the situation is locked in like this. The possibility for dynamic development – be it in the home, work-place or society as a whole – is bound by those confines until something begins to give. Goats, amongst other things, are known for their stubborness. Pan, however, is not all goat.

The human soul is capable of turning to the universal principles that are to be found at its very core, and of these none is more potent than Venus. When we turn to them, the fear that normally traps us within our habitual limits gives way to a far larger world, where love not only becomes the unifying factor but also the creative one.

When love dominates thinking, new ways are found to deal with problems that previously seemed insoluble. When love becomes the true dynamic in the situation, anything is possible.

When Socrates talks about Pan turning words about, he is referring to the thoughts which circle in our heads, thoughts which all of us are subject to, circling thoughts which return to continually impress themselves upon our minds. Through these thoughts all our impressions are filtered. From these thoughts we react to events. They seem to take over and rule our moods, and we can't seem to shake them off. If you don't believe that these circling thoughts control the mind, consider what your mind turns to over and over again.

But love lies beneath all this. Go to the place where the agitations don't afflict, then use what is to be found there to overcome the obstacles that appear in the events you meet. This is the way to transcend limits in both your inner and outer life.

REFLECTION

When confined by negative emotion, ask yourself if you are really these thoughts and emotions that have captivated your heart and mind and become the source of what you say and do. If you conclude that you are not, let them go.

Chapter four

Harmony and repose

Every morning I walk *from the car park to the office. It takes fifteen minutes. In that time my world is what is contained inside my head. For months I haven't seen anything of what's outside myself. Over the last week I made a supreme effort to connect with the senses. For the first time for a long time I saw the streets.*

This was an observation given by someone attending one of the groups I take. It's the kind of observation that is often made because it describes life as most of us experience it. We become locked into habitual ways of behaving. One of those habitual ways is to go over likely events in the day to come, or to tinker with past events, adjusting them to how they should have gone, if only. All this has its own drive, and this drive forces us from the present moment where things are really taking place, where harmony is to be found.

Here is another observation about coming into the moment and finding harmony in it.

On Monday I went into Marks and Spencer's at lunchtime. Everybody was trying to get a sandwich and drinks and to get back to the office as quickly as possible. Everybody seemed to be crowding in on me. It was awful!

Suddenly the whole thing changed. Rather than being caught up in my emotional response, I became strangely detached, and I could see the whole scene before me. It changed everything! Now everybody was moving in harmony. It changed my attitude to the whole day. The experience affected the rest of the week – it carried on.

Why so strangely detached? The reason is simple. Detachment feels strange because it's something we experience rarely. We are normally in a state of total attachment, and who is attached? Me, of course. When we talk of all those people pushing and shoving for their sandwiches, they are the ones who are getting in the way of my sandwiches, who are preventing me from getting back to my office, who are forcing me into my world, dividing me from the rest. And where division is experienced, harmony disappears. Notice what was experienced when the sense of division went: 'Everybody was moving in harmony.'

One of the fears that people have about the sense of detachment is that they will lose their emotional attachment to things. Certainly there is a loss, a loss of emotional commitment to my world and all its claims. There is also a huge gain: an ever-expanding appreciation of things in all their undivided beauty.

PRACTICE

- When you find yourself in a crowded place, in the streets or on a crowded train, everybody appearing to be locked into their own separate world, don't become attached to your own point of pressure.
- Detach yourself and recognize how, outside the realm of the personal, there's a wonderful harmony about what is going on around you.

Repose

Rest and repose are usually considered the preserve of corpses, but repose has its own dynamic, its own vitality. Rest in action allows for possibility. When you see a great sportsman or a dancer, a noticeable thing about them is their sense of ease, that despite the incredible speed and vigour in all that they do, there is also a sense of complete composure.

When you see a great game of any kind, despite all the elation and despondency, there is great pleasure to be gained from seeing the conjunction of movement and rest.

Sportsmen are forever trying to find the space. If they are lucky they can find it out there on the field of play. If they are even luckier, they can also find it within themselves. You can see it clearly as a jumper prepares to jump or as a sprinter gets down on the blocks. You can see it as a footballer takes a corner, ready to curl a ball in, or a rugby player as he prepares to take a conversion. There is a sense of inner stillness and complete concentration. Something like this can be seen in almost every sport. Although straining to the ultimate, some sportsmen – the great ones – possess this power even in the midst of action. It's at the heart of the pleasure we gain from seeing them in full flight. Every action is totally harmonic and utterly economic. In these movements we recognize their intelligence and skill. We describe them as being 'on form'. Their reactions are 'lightning sharp' and yet they have 'all the time in the world'. Why? Because they are physically at their peak. They have a body that is utterly responsive to the requirements of the game and, what is more, they are totally in the moment. This is where 'all the time in the world' exists. This is the eternal present. A game may have been carefully planned, with all kind of strategies developed to beat the opposition, but it's the moment that counts. This magical dimension is where everything is lit, where there exists space and all possibility. It's where maximum action and maximum rest reside. We may not be great sportsmen, but there is nothing stopping us learning from their achievements.

PRACTICE

- Whether in preparation or in play, being in the moment is what counts, utterly alert and utterly at rest. Try it.

Trying to fix the future

Sometimes we entertain the belief that we have to totally envisage the future, run a thousand computer-generated scenarios through our laptops. Although there is nothing wrong in making plans, the best made plans of mice and men often go astray. And it's no good pushing plans through regardless. Circumstances are constantly changing, and the mind, being so infinitely flexible, is quite capable of constantly updating in order to meet the current situation.

Although this is readily acceptable as an idea, because we are subject to fear often we try in some way or another to fix the future. Here, for instance, is a very recognizable observation:

I was offered a new job last week. Suddenly my mind was filled with all the possible things that could go wrong. I remembered that all I needed to see was the next few steps ahead. I was grateful that these things had been offered, both the job and the way to cope with the challenge. The doubts lifted. I found myself doing the next necessary thing, like writing the two pages the job demanded for the following morning. With the memory that I only need to concentrate on immediate requirements and not take on the worry of the entire future, everything works well.

It works because of a paradox. In attending to the next step only instead of envisaging all future possibilities, knowledge of what is really needed is presented in the present. Knowledge cannot arise at any other time than the present. It is here that insight occurs. When there is real penetration the present situation is understood and met, and there is also understanding of future possibilities. Constraining the present by trying to force it into an end dictated by desire closes the situation down and prevents possibilities from manifesting. Even if those possibilities were to manifest, there is every chance of us not recognizing them because they don't fit the preconception. There could be a kind of harmony in events if we could connect with that place from where the harmony is arising. That place is to be found in the present.

- When thoughts of past and future cloud the mind, come into the present.
- Constantly return to the harmony of the here and now.
- The senses are powerful but severely under-used tools. Employ them to the full in the present moment.

Saving sight

Sometimes the physical impairs the senses. Beethoven became deaf. Monet suffered from cataracts, and the vivid world of the garden which he created and painted so beautifully disappeared into a monochrome. Thankfully for him, his sense was restored after a painful operation gave him back his sight, and thereafter he went on to paint some of his greatest masterpieces, the vibrancy of the colour of which he had such an intimate awareness leaping from his canvases. His connection with the visual world of colour and form is obvious. Cézanne said of him: 'Monet is all eye, but what an eye!'

Eye surgery has progressed considerably since Monet's day. I am in contact with an eye surgeon who is using the latest techniques of laser surgery. She talks of what it is like to carry out such delicate operations. She describes how every part of her is dedicated to this one small organ of sight. She herself must have clarity of sight, but not just sight. All her senses are involved in a state of single-pointed attention. They work in perfect harmony, dedicated to the delicate process of saving sight.

In the midst of the operation there are no thoughts of past and future, no worries or concerns. There is only the delicate demand of the present moment. All her knowledge and skill is dedicated to the task. In terms of time and space, this place is small indeed, but in experience it is vast. I asked her about her feelings for her work. She said, 'I absolutely love it.'

This is not an excited kind of love, but it's very deep. The tiny aperture of the eye opens onto a huge world. In her case it is both an inward and an outward opening. It opens onto a world of understanding and compassion. It is this sight that we must develop and, once achieved, preserve.

PRACTICE

- Consider the aperture of the eye, what it is stimulated by. Be conscious of this instrument, so tiny yet encompassing so much – light, shade, colour, form – providing us with our vision of the world. It may focus on something very close to hand or something far in the distance. It even stretches out to infinity. Connect fully with the act of looking. Become still within. Let the agitations of the mind subside, and make full connection with light and shade, colour and form as it falls upon the eye. Be like Monet, conscious of the visual world in all its colour and graphic detail, and like him also, be aware of how all of this detail so perfectly harmonizes.

The eye of the mind

How we see has fascinated us for centuries. Over the last hundred years much has been discovered which before was a complete mystery. For instance, we now know that visual information is brought back to a part of the brain called the 'occipital lobe', and that each eye is connected to a completely separate domain. These domains are in turn divided. One part deals with the information sent in from the rod cells in the eyes, which are highly sensitive to light, enabling us to see in the dimmest conditions. What they don't supply is colour recognition. For this, brighter conditions are required which activate the cone cells. This and much more has been the subject of intensive research.

What hasn't been discovered is the over-arching principle that draws all this discreet information into a unified whole, remembering of course that the sense of sight is not our only sense. You don't have to be an eye surgeon to experience all the senses working in harmony. We may focus on one thing after another, but when we do focus we see a seamless reality, not fragments. Everything harmonizes and creates a single picture of the sensory world.

All the information about what appears to lie beyond us is received by the stimulation of the sensory receptors and conveyed by the nervous system to its own particular home in the brain.

Positron Emission Tomography enables us to detect the brain's electro-chemical responses. What this technique cannot do is shed any light on how stimulation of the brain's nerve cells is finally interpreted and composed into the picture we have of the objective world that lies out there beyond us.

The British physicist, Sir Arthur Eddington, in his book *Beyond the Veil of Physics*, reflected on the organs of sensory perception:

Some influence emanating from it plays on the extremity of a nerve, starting a series of physical and chemical changes which are propagated along the nerve to a brain cell; there a mystery happens, and an image or sensation arises in the mind which cannot purport to resemble the stimulus which excites it. Everything known about the material world must in some way or another have been inferred from these stimuli transmitted along the nerves. It is an astonishing feat of deciphering that we should have been able to infer an orderly scheme of natural knowledge from such indirect communication.

But clearly there is one kind of knowledge which cannot pass through such channels, namely the knowledge of the intrinsic nature of that which lies at the far end of the line of communication.

At the far end of these lines of communication lies the power that informs these brain cells, the power that creates from a multitude of discrete pieces of information a totally unified picture of the world around us.

The eye of the mind, working in all its minute precision, possesses the power to synthesize. Human intelligence is a perfect example of harmonization at work. As we have discussed, to harmonize requires the recognition of parts within the context of the whole, which is exactly what the human mind does. Working from unity in order to establish unity seems central to human intelligence.

PRACTICE

- Follow what the mind does of its own volition.
- Rest with the unity. This can be achieved by simply remembering that which sees as well as that which is seen. Usually we are possessed by the objects of sense – what we see, hear, taste, touch and smell – and forget the still observer which sees all, embraces all, and, being of itself a unity, harmonizes and unifies all. The deeper the appreciation of this underlying observer, the more powerful will be the sense of harmony.

Within the context of the universal

An observation was made to me recently:

You claim your own sufferings or simply deal with them.

How true, for when we claim something we put our own identity, our own limitations upon something that could be met not only within the personal context but also the universal. When there is a connection with the universal, suddenly things are seen in a different light, including our sufferings.

But what is this universal?

The very thing we are exploring, the principle of harmony, is a universal. The following observation arises out of a sense of the universal. It speaks of universality and of harmony. It addresses a personal sorrow within a far larger context than an individual claim on the sorrow experienced:

My grandmother died last week, three years after her husband. She used to say, 'If there's something to be done, do it now.'

I phone my mother every day. She is living in the present dealing with the aftermath of death, looking back to the past in sorrow, but dealing with what's needed in the present.

My brother has a seven month old baby. She's so new, but it's as if she's always been there. 'Waiting to fill it or leave it. That's the cycle of life and death,' was another thing my grandma used to say.

Being alive, we should value the moment.

I am sure all of us have experienced something of what is being alluded to here – a strong sense of the past, sorrow at what has passed, and yet at the same time a vivid sense of the present, and a deep connection with those very qualities embodied in the life being mourned.

On one level these qualities are very particular, very real to us in the nature of that person, but on another level they remain as universals, ready to be adopted by another. 'You fill it, then leave it.' Although life has passed from that person, life does not die, nor, as in this case, does the wisdom expressed in that life. 'If there's something to be done do it now.' And what better thing could we do but accept the wisdom we have been given and come alive to the beauty of this moment?

It would seem from this observation that we can honour the memory of those we love by expressing the same wisdom in our lives that they expressed in theirs. And if what they sought to express were those great universals, like harmony and love, then we can't help but love in turn. We do this by recognizing their presence in the qualities they embodied, as alive in the life being lived now as they were in the life that was lived then.

To express harmony is the best way to celebrate life and those divine forces that find their embodiment in a life well lived.

PRACTICE
- If there's something to be done, do it now. Procrastination creates a dead weight.
- When you leave something that should be addressed now, it becomes much heavier when you next try to pick it up. The life appears to go out of it.
- Acknowledge the natural way of things and working with them

rather than against them. There is no better way of doing this than by giving of yourself and dealing with the need.

The mind is like a lake

The mind is like a lake and every stone that drops into it raises waves. These waves do not let us see what we are. The full moon is reflected in the lake, but the surface is so disturbed that we do not see the reflection clearly. Let it be calm. Do not let nature raise the wave. Keep quiet and then after a little while she will give you up.

In this quotation from the Indian philosopher, Vivikenanda, he is recommending a reflective way of life. Notice what he identifies as disturbing this reflection: the waves. When we are in a state of continual agitation, how might we find some rest from it? With this rest comes peace, tranquillity, calm. Depth also comes with it: 'Still waters run deep.' But waters can only be seen to be deep when they are still. Agitations on the surface prevent recognition. Look down into the still waters of the lake and there is a chance of seeing the depths, throw a rock in and there's no chance at all.

With still water there is knowledge of depth. With still water there is also light. It's only still water that may reflect the moonlight, sunlight, or, for that matter, any kind of light.

Agitations prevent all this. They also, according to Vivikenanda, prevent us from discovering who we really are. For self-knowledge we need stillness of mind and inner illumination. That is why methods which encourage the mind to become still and lit go by the general name of reflection. The light of understanding arises only when the agitations of the mind fall still. The problem is that the mind is most agitated when understanding is most needed. This is why we have to constantly adopt a reflective state of mind. We have to train the mind to be in command of itself and not be possessed by events.

Turn to the next practice particularly when you are in the midst of agitation.

PRACTICE

- Consciously adopt a reflective state of mind.
- Consciously return to the stillness over and over again.
- Be aware of the light and the depth that is in everything.

Being given back to yourself

If by Rudyard Kipling remains one of the most popular poems in the English language; judging from the annual polls, the most popular. Why? Because it speaks of what we are discussing here. It takes the form of advice given by a father to his son.

> *If you can keep your head when all about you*
> *Are losing theirs and blaming it on you.*
> *If you can trust yourself when all men doubt you,*
> *But make allowances for their doubting too:*
> *If you can wait and not be tired of waiting.*
> *Or being lied about, don't deal in lies.*
> *Or being hated, don't give way to hating,*
> *And yet don't look too good, nor talk too wise*

The poet suggests that after all this and much more is achieved only then would his son become a man.

It is not so much a matter of the possession of human consciousness that separates us from the beasts, but, according to this way of thinking, more the ability to utilize the consciousness we have been given so as to remain calm and centred in the face of all kinds of adversity.

It would seem that the more life creates agitation, the more there is a desire for this inner stillness, if only as a form of relief. This surely is the mind's innate understanding of itself and its deep-rooted needs. The only problem is that unless the forms exist in society for this need to be met, the desire itself becomes another form of mental agitation.

If, however, we go back to Vivikenanda, we discover that the way forward is to use reflection in the pursuit of self-knowledge. He suggests that, by adopting forms of reflection, things that normally create agitation no longer have the power they once had. He speaks of us being given back to ourselves and not wrenched away by the events of life.

As we have already mentioned more than once, it's the inner connection that creates peace of mind. The less we know of ourselves, the more agitated we become, and the more agitated we become, the less we know of ourselves. This creates a downward spiral of discord and lack of love.

The direction in which we are being pointed is evident. In the midst of this whirl of events we call 'my life', we must find time to fall still and reflect our own inner light. If the forms that will allow us to do this do not readily exist, we can do no better than follow the practices in this book.

PRACTICE

- Do not let nature raise the wave, nor your nature nor anybody else's.
- When you feel your stomach muscles tightening and your temper beginning to rise, don't go with it. This isn't you that's under attack. There's something, deeper, stiller and brighter to be known.
- Never merely react. Act from that inner knowledge instead.

The light of understanding

When we talk of the light of understanding, we see that light in terms of the thing we are trying to understand rather than the light itself. When the light dawns, things are lit up for us, but that by which we understand remains a mystery.

This may well be the case, but what we might do is live in the memory of this light and not allow ourselves to be forever totally involved by what the light illuminates.

Sometimes we catch a glimpse of this light, reflected like the full moon in a still lake. It's there to be found in all those things that attract the senses, even the things that may well have possessed us in the past, but now have drawn us into a deeper sense of connection. They have a lightness and beauty that we might not have noticed before. They may possess that sense of harmony of which we have been speaking. It would certainly be true to say that we feel a harmony with whatever it is that has touched us in this way, a sense of unity. Even the most mundane things may catch us unawares with their light. This is not some kind of garish outer glamour sucking us in, but a quiet presence.

Here is an example of what I mean, provided by a young businesswoman who told me of a particular experience:

I was standing in a very crowded city street in the pouring rain. The road was full of traffic, and the pavements were crowded with people hurrying by. I stopped for a moment and glanced down and was struck by the beauty of this single paving stone, which seemed to have lain there unnoticed for so long. Amidst all the noise and the bustle, I thought that this single stone was a kind of sanctuary. Then I looked up and realized that the enduring patience that I'd seen in the stone was in fact everywhere, underlying all the noise and bustle.

PRACTICE

- Even the most mundane things may provide the opportunity for connection. Don't dismiss them. By dismissing them they become mundane.
- Look for the beauty in everything.

Train the mind to remember

Where is the light that shows us beauty? It's there all the time. The bustle of the city streets is empowered by that same energy. This energy is used up in the thrust of life. It is used to drive us across the surface. These are the waves, but beneath the waves lie the still bright depths, 'the enduring patience' that is there all along, unnoticed.

It has remained unnoticed because the still bright depths that lie in our own minds beneath the agitations of thought also remain unnoticed. This is the same energy manifesting in all its purity and calm, not scattered by the agitations of life.

Here is another example:

We had been out to Kent for a drive in the country. It had been a beautiful day, and now in the early evening we were making our way back into London.

We got on to the top of the North Downs where there is a fine view over the Weald of Kent. I decided that it would be nice to stop the car and have a look.

We clambered over this fence into a field that sloped steeply away. There it was, the Weald, an expanse of farmland stretching out to the horizon, where a beautiful sunset could be seen.

Suddenly I became aware that there were other people in the field, all silently sitting, watching the sunset. I was unnerved for a moment, but that passed.

It was beautiful. There was no doubt, but the question came to mind. 'Where is the beauty?'

It seemed a silly question, because the beauty could be seen everywhere. Everybody was sitting in silent recognition of it, but the question pressed, and I looked hard at all the beautiful things in an attempt to find an answer, but no matter how hard I looked, I couldn't see it, not the real beauty. It seemed to elude me.

But after a while I slowly became aware that the beauty I was seeking for so hard was to be found nowhere but in my own consciousness of beauty.

That seemed strange enough, but then it dawned that this consciousness was not just my consciousness, for everybody that was there, everything that was there, the people on the hillside, the whole landscape and the sunset beyond seemed to be held in the same consciousness. The forms were but the outer manifestation of something that lay behind everything, both inner and outer.

Sometimes experiences of this nature come unbidden. Once they have come, they are not easily forgotten. What I am suggesting, however, is that through the spirit of love these deeper insights into the nature of things may not be a matter of mere chance. They may be consciously sought for even in the midst of life's physical and emotional turmoil, in the midst of those situations that can easily possess us entirely. But in order to seek them, we must train the mind to remember.

PRACTICE

- Live more deeply by not being attracted and agitated by what lies on the surface.
- Don't be so keen to be dragged into whatever is captivating people's minds at the present. Look out for what endures and unites. This has its own profound beauty and is the source of harmony and repose.

The pleasures of solitude

Later in the book we will consider 'The End of Separation'. What follows could very well fit that context. It also beautifully expresses the joy of being in harmony with things, of living more deeply. It is an extract from an essay on 'The Pleasures of Solitude' written by an eleven-year-old boy from a class I take. He is by nature a very robust, athletic sort of boy, certainly not the introverted, retiring type, and yet ... Read on and see what you think.

The life I lead is full of people; brimming with brothers, sisters, friends and more. But when I need rest, or when life has really put its yoke on my neck, then I must be alone. Solitude quietens me down and then brings me totally to my senses, and everything gently simmers down into a pool of freshness.

But many would prefer to rush out and join the throng of life, and collect friends, and take them out into a waiting world of cinemas and throbbing strobe lights.

But no, that life is not for me. The lights just give me headaches, and I see my friends at school.

I like to be alone, where there is nothing to disturb the quiet. Solitude is a chance to open out in the swing of nature. Dark damp forests, lush green grass, splinters of light falling through a country glade, all can be enjoyed, but if you are alone with them, they become part of you. You can feel the way trees feel, swaying in the wind, and you know all you need to know.

The place solitude tugs most at my head, though, is its inner world.

There lies complete stillness, like a restful pool of tranquil water in the burning heat of day. And as I lower myself into this pool I feel the pleasures of solitude rush around me, and it is then that I realise, and acknowledge with my full heart, that solitude is not loneliness. For I am not lonely when I am alone and without a fellow companion, and I like it that way.

This does not mean that I do not enjoy my friends' company. Of course I do. But it is solitude I desire most, and I expect it will always be so.

His thoughts express something I am sure that all of us have experienced and valued. As it won a national competition, it was evident that the judges recognized this universality too.

The Romantics called this experience 'communing with nature', but it's clear from the essay that it's the inner world where the communion really takes place. The outer serves as the herald of the inner, the means by which the connection is made. At moments like this, we come to our own inner self, and know all we need to know. This is self-knowledge, the source of true contentment.

PRACTICE

- Acknowledge the presence of your inner self.
- Despite all the outer activities in your life, be sure to find rest in what is there. Turn to it whenever you remember, even in the midst of action.

Chapter five

Venus within

THERE IS NO DOUBT that the Venus we are discussing in this book is not some antique myth but a living principle which is here with us as a fundamental feature of our lives. We have been discovering something of the nature of this goddess in both her material and sublime forms. We have gone some way to awakening her presence. But what more might we do to bring her fully into our lives?

She is not some fanciful notion that we are toying with, picked up only to be put down again. If the goddess lives within us, we must remember her, consciously enter her precinct and deliberately connect with her presence.

But where does she live and how might we get in touch?

All the places that the poets describe, her sacred grove, her temple, are but symbols of her traditional home, the human soul. Our task is to turn to the soul and kindle this principle of love. But there are certain difficulties attached.

> *We cannot kindle when we will*
> *The fire which in the heart resides,*
> *The spirit bloweth and is still,*
> *In mystery our soul abides.*

Here is the Victorian poet Matthew Arnold, in a poem called *Morality*, expressing the mystery of the soul. For over a hundred years the soul's action and location has been more than a mystery.

Its domain has been taken over by the psyche, a term of long lineage and rich with meaning, but with its use the significance of the word 'soul' has drifted out of our consciousness.

When soul is combined with heart – heart and soul – a sense of what this means registers; heartlessness and soullessness are ways of being we easily recognize. We certainly know what a dead, soulless environment feels like, and we are aware of an emotional response to it. We do have a kind of understanding. But notions such as 'care of the soul', the 'enlargement of the soul' have drifted into obscurity in our predominantly materialistic view.

There are, of course, people who are far from soulless. They are living proof of the soul's existence. If the thinkers of the classical world are anything to go by, recognized or not, none of us is free from the promptings of the soul. There are times when our hearts are lifted and times when they are made heavy, depressed. Wordsworth speaks of 'dull souls', as those who are untouched by beauty, and sometimes that is exactly the condition of our souls; nothing seems capable of lifting our spirits. It is also the condition of the soul untouched by love. Our object in this book is to deny Matthew Arnold's claim and to unveil the mystery of the soul and kindle the flame of love.

PRACTICE

• Choose a task, the simpler the better, and consciously dedicate yourself to it heart and soul.

The soul's domain

Jesse, who was mentioned previously, lived appropriately enough at the Sun Inn. Apollo is the god of the sun. He is the god of healing, master of music and poetry. One may look upon this book as being a means of introducing the 'Jesse Factor' into our lives by awakening the soul, by healing the soul and by educating the soul in its essential harmony. At the heart of Jesse's life, which wasn't without its difficulties, was the overriding spirit of love, a spirit that encompassed all those who came into her company. You had to work hard to resist it. It was around this central principle that all her other qualities revolved and into which her friends were naturally drawn.

As we shall discover later, the spirit of love and the spirit of healing are closely related. According to the soul-related philosophy of the Renaissance, the human soul, Humanitas, and the spirit of love, Venus, were the same thing, and in order to act in a way that was truly humane one had to act in the spirit of love.

But what is not easily recognized or accepted by modern minds is the extent of soul. If we do think of soul at all, we think of it as somehow locked inside our bodies. So called 'traditional wisdom' talks of the *anima mundi*, the 'soul of the world'. According to this way of thinking, soul is universal as well as individual.

If that is too hard a concept to grasp, consider this. Much of what is being explored here is born out by experience. The individuals whose observations are given are certainly affected by their insights, but also, necessarily, are all the other people with whom they have come in contact. We have our private worlds in which we carry our individual qualities intact, but we are also affected by others and have the power to affect in turn. Not only people but places as well may dramatically affect our experience of life. Why do we go to such great lengths to escape the city, in order to seek the tranquility of the countryside? We are trying to restore our souls. The idea of home has at its core the idea of rest and restoration. Why is the idea of going home so utterly appealing?

PRACTICE

- Humanitas = Venus. Reflect on these words as separate concepts and then draw them into one.

Subtle worlds

A vivid example of this shift of substance comes readily to mind. It took place on a visit I made to the church of San Miniato al Monte. This church was built in 1018 over the shrine of an early Christian martyr, Saint Minias. It is one of the most beautiful and unspoiled of all the Romanesque churches in Italy, and has two additional virtues. It stands on a hill high above Florence. The views from the terrace outside the church are stunning. More importantly, it is the church for a monastic order that has been in existence since it was built. The spirit of devotion is palpable.

The day I last went there coincided with a visit by a group of Italian teenagers whose tour of the church had ended. As I arrived they were occupying themselves playing football on the sun-burnt terrace outside the West door. Their devotion to the game was total and infectious. Their voices, echoing off the façade of the church, filled the place with vitality.

On entering the church, the contrast could not have been more stark. Even before my eyes became accustomed to the darkness, the silence was striking. It was if the church held a quality that was not being detected by any of the physical senses but was readily recognized none the less. It overwhelmed whatever I had brought with me.

As my eyes adjusted, the beauty of the church revealed itself, and then in the distance I could hear the sound of plainsong, possessing its own spiritual beauty. What was now being conveyed to my senses did not in any way disturb what was originally known but instead seemed to magnify it. What was also magnified was my inner perception, which recognized the atmosphere of the church before anything of its physical nature was known. In fact the beauty of the physical forms of the church – not only the architectural forms, the paintings and sculpture, but also the words and music of the liturgy – seemed to have its conception in that quality which was known from the very beginning: the soul of the place.

When we fully connect with anything of abiding beauty it is not a process in which we tick off the parts according to some intellectual system. Beauty has its own immediacy and its own totality. The atmosphere of beauty is something to which the soul cannot help but respond. It cannot help but respond because the soul's fundamental nature is being evoked.

And what is this atmosphere? Is it both individual and general at the same time? Does it both affect us physically and psychologically at the same time? Is it both inner and outer at the same time?

We would not recognize the presence of beauty if the principle of beauty was not already present within us. The presence of beauty as recognized through the senses evokes the presence of beauty held within.

PRACTICE

- Consider something that you find beautiful.
- Consider the parts that add to its beauty, then reflect on its beauty as a whole.

Tuning in

The quality of love stilleth our will, and
maketh us long for what we have,
and giveth no other thirst.

DANTE, *Paradiso* III 70

Consider again what you have been influenced by in your life and to what extent you have influenced others. Consider the nature of that influence. Ideas must certainly influence, but what of the emotional ground from which those ideas arise?

In considering these questions, we are beginning to detect the realm of the soul. And we are beginning to see soul in each other, in our activities and surroundings. It's as if we are tuning into our own souls, and in the process allowing this whole realm to expand because our knowledge of it is growing. We are no longer merely occupying our own private space. We are turning out, looking out, and our hearts are going out. What we are entering is the realm of the soul, and in the process we are being given the chance to become great souls, *magna anima*. This is from where we get our word 'magnanimity'. Magnanimity, compassion, charity – these are all powers intimately related to the Venus Principle.

With this awareness there must arise a sense of expansion. There comes a recognition that the soul is not locked inside our bodies, that the soul encompasses the body, not the other way around. When we talk of looking into our own souls, examining our own hearts, when we speak of insight, we are not talking about going into our bodies. We are talking about entering that world which lies at the heart and surrounds this tangible world detected by the senses. This is known as the subtle world. It's within and surrounding this world in which we live. When we touch on those profound principles that live at the heart of this world, when they become manifest in our lives, we can't help but pass them on. If the soul is bigger than the body, then we must be spreading our influence all the time. The body may have its physical limits, but the soul interpenetrates.

PRACTICE

- Remember the nature of influence.
- Be aware of the influences affecting us, from where they come and what their qualities are.

Out of touch and out of tune

In the normal run of events we are unaware of the world of the soul because of our locked-in condition. We are not only locked into our bodies, but also our thinking processes, part of which – recognized or not – tells us there is an external world of so called objective reality and an internal world of so called subjective impression and, according to this way of thinking, if anything remotely like soul exists at all, it's part of this vague subjectivity. The physical is the real world, therefore the body must be real and the mind not so real, and yet while this attitude towards things is in place it is being held by nothing but a set of ideas, subtle forms which influence our whole view of life.

These ideas certainly have their effect. They lock us into our own physical set up and divide us from each other. Under these conditions our experience must be to some extent bound by the physical impression of things. This is the material world in which we try to make our way. Recognizing only the material, this is the level on which we operate. Because the promptings of the soul are denied, our abilities to connect with those principles held in the soul are greatly hindered. Wordsworth expresses this state of the soul perfectly:

> *The world is too much with us; late and soon,*
> *Getting and spending, we lay waste our powers,*
> *Little we see in Nature that is ours;*
> *We have given our hearts away, a sordid boon!*
> *This sea that bares its bosom to the moon;*
> *The wind that will be howling at all hours,*
> *And are up-gathered now like sleeping flowers;*
> *For this for everything, we are out of tune;*
> *It moves us not.*

Here is the state that we must have all experienced: out of touch, out of tune, somehow denied something that is central to our experience as human beings. The beauty of the world is lost to us, and we seem unable to properly relate to others. And yet, at other times, we have no problem in relating. It seems as if the ability is given to us quite naturally.

There are, of course, some amongst us who have the ability to be in touch as a constant in their lives. They possess subtle understanding, and out of compassion hold others in their being. Jesse was a perfect example of this, and all of us have come across people like her.

After all what else do we want from any loving relationship but some kind of mutual expansion in which both are encompassed?

What else do we want in our relationship with the world around us but a totality of experience which is full and deep and that doesn't leave us isolated and alone?

By considering these questions we are inevitably led to a greater understanding of the soul and the principles that exist within the soul, the principles that unite us all, none more fundamental than the Principle of Love.

PRACTICE

- Ask yourself this question: What is it that at any one time cuts me off? Whenever the sense of isolation manifests in any way, pose this question again.

The divided self

In Plato's *Symposium* all the guests take it in turn to talk about the nature of love. When it comes to Aristophanes' turn to speak, he retells a myth related to the nature of the soul and of love. It's an amusing story as befits the greatest comedy writer of the classical world.

He speaks of how mankind was not originally as we find ourselves at present. Once mankind appeared round and whole with backs and the sides formed into a circle, four hands and legs and two faces joined at the neck.

These round people were very proud of themselves, so much so that they wanted to take on the gods. Zeus, in order to put them in their place, got hold of them and sliced them down the middle like hard-boiled eggs, promising that if they were ever again to rise up in pride against the gods he would slice them into quarters.

After they were chopped up in this way they were cast out, and each half desperately sought its other half. In their passionate desire to return to their former condition, whenever they met they would run towards one another and embrace. Having found their wholeness, Aristophanes claims that men were blessed.

We are still left with a remnant of this famous myth with phrases such as 'a marriage made in heaven' or 'my other half' and sometimes even 'my better half'. In his interpretation of Aristophanes' contribution, Ficino, in his book *On Love*, reflects upon the myth. He says these divided creatures are not in fact two but represent aspects of our divided selves. Our souls are created whole and possess two lights, one originating within us, and one poured into us. We employ the innate light to see things equal or inferior to us, and with the infused light we see that which is superior.

Although the innate light is of vital importance, allowing us to find our way about the physical world, when we employ it alone and become unconscious of the infused light, certain things must inevitably follow. We seek lasting happiness in physical things, which by their very nature are subject to change. In this we are bound to be frustrated, but instead of giving up we are driven all the stronger in the pursuit of novelty, new possessions, new sensations. We become possessed by passing pleasure.

The other limiting factor of this light is that, being innate, it appears to be our own. Something that is infused must come from somewhere else. Inspiration is breathed into us. If we are intent on using what appears to be ours only, then the possibility of something coming from without is rejected. If by chance something does slip through, then it is either claimed as a personal possession or rejected as mere fancy.

And who remains at the centre of this appreciation of life? Me. In this there lies a fundamental duality – me and the rest. This belief lies at the heart of all our inevitable desires and frustrations. Love, which by its very nature is unified in origin and expression, is the complete opposite to this state of division and separation.

Through the force of our egotism we rise a second time against the gods and are quartered. In this we risk losing the infused light altogether and with it our awareness of beauty. There is nothing remotely physical about beauty, for that which we call physical beauty can only be recognized when the infused light of beauty rises within us to meet that which evokes it.

When nothing seems beautiful and the whole world seems grey, then we can be sure that the infused light which allows insight to operate is no longer functioning. Ego has had its way.

However, when the intuitive appreciation of that infused light starts to stir once more, the quest for that half of ourselves that we have subconsciously ignored may reassert itself.

In this context Venus is none other than the desire that leads us to search for our own totality and the joy that is felt when any sense of it is discovered.

The function of true philosophy and true art is to help us in this search.

PRACTICE

- What is it that illuminates all my senses: seeing, hearing, touching, tasting?
- What illuminates my deepest thoughts?
- Before reacting to what life presents, be aware that consciousness illuminates all.

The light flow

Those people we come across who possess a sense of harmony and happiness, who find it easy to love, are in some way, to some extent, in touch with that infused light, and have linked up with an element of that divine aspect of themselves.

Before pursuing this any further, let us return to the notion of overlapping souls. If our souls are indeed far larger than our bodies, how easily will the principle of love, once discovered – in the way that these people so obviously have discovered it – flow?

Our task is a simple one: to recognize the presence of the principle of love, magnify her presence by consciously devoting our actions to her, and then pass on her presence, which we can't but help do if we have faith in her existence.

Each of us must judge according to experience, but there can be experience of nothing without the organs of perception to enable the experience to take place. You can attune your ears. Taste and touch can be made more sensitive. By training, you can become more aware of colour and form. All kinds of mental facilities can be developed. In the same way, the subtle organs of perception that surround the Principle of Love may also be developed. The gods don't come unless invited, but, once invited, who knows what might transpire.

Wordsworth concludes the poem we considered earlier in this chapter still looking out over the beauty of the sea, pleading to see the gods of the ancient world, his poetic expression speaking of the powers of the soul. Without these powers he is 'forlorn'. Forlorn means forsaken, deprived of love. The poem is an expression of his desire to make connection with those powers.

If, by our actions, we were to make our own connection with those things all of us possess, we too would find the 'inward happiness' that Wordsworth says he seeks, and we would, moreover, be able to pass it on.

PRACTICE
- Recognize the presence of the principle of love.
- Magnify her presence by consciously devoting your actions to her, and then pass on her presence.

The forms of love

In looking back and remembering those whom we have loved and who have loved us, there must be a recognition that their influence, although long past, remains. Their presence has not been in any way diminished by the passage of time. Just considering them is a way of allowing them once more to enter our lives, bringing with them the love that allowed them to have such a powerful influence.

It was not for nothing that Plato wanted others to come to a proper understanding of the nature of beauty and love. Throughout the Dialogues he speaks of turning from the world of constant change, our normal experience of life, to that place of constancy and purity. In this state we may be true to ourselves rather than be battered by events, one thing one moment and another the next. By connecting with the eternal principles, we must of necessity come out of perplexity and depression. Only by so doing can the true nature of the soul be discovered, and only in this discovery may we taste wisdom.

The more of us who become true lovers, the more the spirit of love will spread. Consider what might happen if, in our ordinary everyday lives, in what we surround ourselves by, physically and subtly, there were devotion to Venus. How would our experience of life be transformed, and not just for us personally but for all those with whom we come in contact? If enough people were to experience the principle of love as a constant in their lives, were to devote themselves to its presence, there may well form a critical mass, a force that would overflow into the community at large. Then the general experience of this material world with all its tensions and conflicting claims would transform itself, and we would see it as a direct expression of the ideal world of which Plato speaks.

This is the way it has always been. Recognition of this has been expressed over and over again. It is only by the aid of these ideals that civilizations are formed. The way we measure the greatness of a civilization is through the beauty of its architecture, the beauty of its art, the justice of its laws and the profundity of its poetry and philosophy. All these things are devoted to the eternal principles. In our recognition of them we give the powers permission to operate through us. Only in our devotions do the forms of love arise.

One of the most beautiful vows of love is to be found, not

surprisingly, in the most famous of all love stories, Shakespeare's *Romeo and Juliet*. In three terse lines of poetry, a small compressed form, Juliet expresses the totality and universality of love:

> *My bounty is as boundless as the sea,*
> *My love as deep: the more I give to thee,*
> *The more I have: for both are infinite.*

PRACTICE

- Think about these three lines, and then practise them – creatively, in ways entirely suited to the situation.

Love comes at no other time but now

In Renaissance art Venus is often pictured in a spring garden, symbol of rebirth and new possibilities. The paintings are full of flowers and trees in new leaf, nature in full flood. This undoubtedly makes the artist's composition all the more attractive, but that's not the real point. The spring imagery is describing how things actually work. Our experience of love may come and go, but there is never a winter of love.

What come and go are the ideas that dominate the mind. Words are creative. They create the confines. They can also create the freedom. When Venus becomes the perpetual point of reference, she has her effect. It draws us into the present where we see things as if for the first time. The manipulations and machinations, the lies and deceit effectively separate us from the knowledge being presented now, and are projections from my past into my future.

Now or never. You must live in the present, launch yourself on every wave, find your eternity in each moment. Fools stand on an island of opportunity and look towards another land.

The New England philosopher Thoreau spells out unequivocally the importance of freeing ourselves from the thrall of past and future. Past regrets and future fears isolate us from the beauty to be found in the present moment. He also speaks of the satisfaction and inspiration to be found in common things, of dreaming of 'no heaven but that which lies about me'.

The most obvious effect of trying to constantly manipulate events in accordance with some private end is that the agitations of mind this effort generates isolate us from the simple beauty to be found when entering deeply into the joy of the present moment, the source of all creativity.

What greater fear could there be than to arrive at the end of our lives only to realize with great regret that we weren't around when it took place, and were somehow separated from life's vivid beauty? Perhaps, after all, fear and regret do have their part to play, if only to encourage us to live now, when life happens.

PRACTICE

- Ask yourself where you are looking. If it's somewhere else than the present need or the present beauty, redirect your eyes and refocus your thoughts.

'Enjoy, do not covet'

A number of years ago I worked for a time as an actor. I was touring in Shakespeare's *Richard II*. The company was due to perform at a festival in Lincolnshire. The man behind the festival was a very successful farmer, a most remarkable man in his way. At the end of our contribution to the festival, he held a dinner party for us in his beautiful Georgian home. Lincolnshire is very flat, and his house was built on the only hill for miles around.

After dinner I wandered out onto the terrace. It was dusk, there was a beautiful sky, and the land stretched out before me. Although I could hear the noise of the others coming through the French windows, what I was mainly aware of was the quiet and the space.

Our host came out and joined me, and we stood for a while

looking out over that fenland country. Then he turned to me and said, 'The whole of that, as far as you can see, belongs to me.'

I remember thinking at the time, 'In one sense', somewhat ironically as it transpired.

He went on speaking. 'My father was a farm labourer, and when I was a boy I used to come and stand at the bottom of the drive and look up at this house, and I thought then, "One day that's going to be mine." Now it's mine and all the land surrounding.'

'It's very beautiful,' I said.

He stopped and looked for a moment, and then said with considerable feeling: 'The whole thing's beautiful.' We stood for a while in silence, looking out, before finally going back to join the others.

The following day we were shocked to hear that the farmer had been killed in a car crash. I remember thinking at the time about the real nature of ownership, and, if any of us owned anything, it was owned in moments like the one I shared with him whilst standing on the terrace.

When finally obtaining something we hold dear, there is always a shadow that accompanies our achievement, the fear of losing it. What is evident from the farmer's situation is that, in any event, we lose it all in the end. Whatever we manage to obtain in life is there on loan, and there is no use in hanging on to it. Live this life, certainly, play your part with a totality of focus and commitment, but you can only really enjoy what life offers you by, in turn, offering the whole thing up and not trying to grapple it to yourself, for in so doing not only do you bind the situation, preventing its proper development and full fruition, you bind yourself and prevent the possibility of any true enjoyment of the very thing you wish to possess.

In one of the great keys to the unlocking of love, the *Eesha Upanishad*, amongst much of great wisdom, offers these simple words: 'Enjoy. Do not covet.' If we could live our lives with that simple advice in mind, then we would be granted a sense of true ownership and lack of fear.

PRACTICE

- Remember the words, 'Enjoy. Do not covet.'

Chapter six

Beauty heals

T HAT GREAT ARTIST AND SCIENTIST, Leonardo da Vinci stated that the soul is by nature harmonious. This is not what most people experience. Having over the last two chapters established our connection with the principle of harmony, we are now going to look more closely at the effect this connection has on mind and body, what happens when there is an apparent lack of harmony, when we are more out of tune than out of salts.

There is no doubt that we live in a time where tension, both personal and social, is having its effect. Here are some indicators of its effects, according to official figures recently published in Britain: 20 per cent of the population suffer from depression, 15 per cent suffer from obsessions and phobias, 10 per cent are addicted to drugs and alcohol, 35 per cent go regularly to their doctors for tranquillizers. An estimated £11 billion is lost annually through stress-related illnesses.

All this indicates a considerable amount of disquiet generally, a lack of harmony and repose. We may not be afflicted with the degree of 'dis-ease' which Ophelia claims Hamlet is suffering from when she speaks of his 'sovereign reason, like sweet bells jangled, out of tune and harsh'; and his 'unmatched form and feature ... blasted with ecstasy ...', but there is much to suggest from even a cursory awareness of the events that are reported on a daily basis in the papers that being 'blasted with ecstasy' isn't that uncommon an occurrence.

All of us, I am sure, looking at our own lives, have met discord and can point to some of its causes. These are many and varied. There are none of us who will have passed through life without experiencing suffering of some sort, and it would certainly be the wrong approach to tranquillize ourselves against it. But there is measure in all things, even in suffering, and when we become possessed by suffering, particularly of the self-inflicted kind, then we must take steps to counter it. There is no better way of dealing with suffering than to appeal to the principle of love.

Hamlet does the opposite, for he has first to reject and then finally destroy what was for him the embodiment of Venus, Ophelia – the one true love of his life – when, out of an overpowering sense of sorrow and loss, he follows a path of destructive revenge.

Love may manifest with a sense of striking particularity, and we become possessed by our devotions – overjoyed when our love is reciprocated and utterly dismayed when it is denied. When we lose those things to which we have become devoted, the suffering can be intense. But love is not only particular; it is also universal, and, as we have already learnt, the nature of universal love is of utmost importance to Socrates and Plato.

The principle of love was paramount in the Christian concept that came to be known as 'care of the soul'. The need for our souls to be cared for in our own times has in many ways intensified. The indicators already quoted are proof enough of this.

PRACTICE

- When sorrows multiply, recognize that love is not only particular but also universal. There is no better way of discovering this than by giving what you lack. If it's love you lack, be sure to give that above anything else.

Holding on to the principle of love

Outside the context of universal love, sorrow has no real significance and may eventually turn into a form of self-indulgence. Love
not only provides the context for sorrow but also the measure. If
that measure is exceeded, then what was pure and selfless becomes
cloying. Within the context of love, sorrow is ennobling, providing
a means of touching the universal nature of things, enabling us to
recognize our lives as part of the play of principles. In this process
harmony is discovered.

This way of thinking has nothing to do with existential misery
and everything to do with nobility of mind. At the time unhappi-
ness strikes this may be difficult to achieve, but it's worth persever-
ing with. Listen to this beautiful description of what might happen
when these principles are put into practice.

*I had to phone my ex-boyfriend. Although we had parted I still knew there
were feelings for him.*

*A woman came on the phone. She sounded very self-assured – as if she
lived there and was comfortable. Inside I froze, but outwardly I spoke in my
most pleasant voice. I was telling myself to be calm.*

*When he came on the phone he was nervous and said he would call
back. When I put down the phone I cried. I thought, 'It's really over.' I was
having a whole dialogue with myself. Then I composed myself. I wanted to
be in a calm state before he phoned back. I came into the present. I didn't
want to be upset and spiteful. I asked myself, 'What is it you are trying to
hold onto? He's already gone.'*

*When he did ring we had a good conversation. I then asked, 'Was that
your new relationship?' He said it was.*

*I then said, 'I hope you will be really happy,' and I meant it. He was very
quiet as if he didn't know how to react. We said good-bye.*

*I made a cup of tea and looked out of the window. I was at peace.
Everything had been resolved. Everything was calm. I was happy. I had
expressed my love.*

PRACTICE

- When sorrow is felt, accept it, but follow it back to its source: the still compassionate nature of love.
- Hold the principle of love in mind. Return to it over and over again, especially when all the emotional involvements return, then allow its pure and all-embracing nature to heal the sorrow. When the measure is reached, turn outwards.
- Meet the need in whatever practical way that need might manifest. Get on with life.

Consciously recognize harmony

Having touched on a kind of sorrow that has an obvious legitimacy, let us now consider things that seem to afflict us for no good or substantial reason. Some have called this the pain of living. There have been many diagnoses over the last 100 years or so as to why we should be subject to this pain. I would like to offer another explanation, one that accords perfectly with the traditional wisdom we have been considering in this book and does not draw its legitimacy from current thinking.

According to traditional wisdom the pain of living stems not so much from sexual frustration, as has been often claimed in our post-Freudian times, but from the soul being out of tune with her higher nature. It's not physical love we lack, more spiritual. Socrates states that, when we are possessed by material concerns, the soul staggers to and fro like a drunkard and is thrown into a state of agitation.

In the Renaissance philosopher Ficino's commentary on the *Symposium*, he tells us that the soul is out of tune because it has become totally involved with concerns of a physical nature. As a result of this its higher parts are almost asleep; the lower parts dominate the others. The former parts are affected by indolence and the latter by agitation. The whole soul is filled with discord and disharmony.

We appear, according to this diagnosis, to be so possessed by the pressures of daily living that the connection with the underlying harmony that Leonardo considers to be the soul's true nature is lost and forgotten. If this does prove to be the case, perhaps Ficino might provide us with a remedy. He was, after all, not only a philosopher, combining knowledge of the traditions of wisdom with inspired insight into its contemporary relevance. He was also the doctor to the Medicis. If anyone might tell us something about the healing of the body and soul, it should be him. He suggests a cure which, on the face of it, appears to be far from rational but might be worthy of consideration.

First, there is a need for poetic madness, which through musical sounds arouses the parts of the soul that are asleep, through harmonious sweetness calms those which are perturbed, and finally – through consonance of diverse things – drives away dissonant discord and tempers the various parts of the soul.

According to this way of thinking, the task is first to arouse the soul from its self-imposed sleep by the power of harmony contained in words and music. This is certainly an imaginative approach to health care. The interesting thing is that he is not the only one to think in this way. There has been a great tradition of care for the body through care of the soul. Today, with ever-increasing attention being paid to preventative medicine, the division between the two is becoming less distinct. The idea of a healthy mind and body is taking on a new meaning, one more in line with the thoughts of Ficino and all those doctors of philosophy and medicine that went before him.

There is now a growing recognition that the body is not a crude mechanism, but is endowed with a subtle intelligence that permeates the whole of its fabric. There is also acceptance that this intelligence, like all forms of intelligence, can become dulled and distorted, and, out of this dullness and distortion, may arise disease.

In order to counter this negative effect, we must learn how to bring the body into tune, because, like any instrument, it needs tuning. We do this by nourishing the body and mind with the finest food in order that this immensely intelligent mechanism may work freely and with its natural precision.

PRACTICE

- Take time to connect with something harmonious. This may be as readily to hand as the wind blowing in the trees, the one giving way to the other. It may be the play of light or the movement of sound.
- Resist the temptation to be carried away into your own dream world of associations and pay attention to the play of the voices, the way they divide or echo one another or come back together to join in unison.
- Listen to the way discord resolves into harmony, all the parts, whether harmonious or discordant, arising out of the totality of the composition.
- Consciously recognize harmony.

Mind healing

So where does the idea of beauty healing come in? It's not a new idea. The Greeks entertained the simple idea that beauty heals. They believed that beauty has the power to bring the discordant elements of the mind and body into a loving accord, and this principle of love they called 'Eros'.

Under the authority of Asklepios, the Greek god of healing, whose wand remains the symbol of the healing arts, his followers conducted a form of health-care called 'Nootherapia', or mind healing, which sought to bring the mind and body under the health-giving power of harmony.

One of the great sites of classical culture, Epidauros, was entirely devoted to this idea. It was a centre of art and medicine. People went there to find harmony of body and soul. They sought to be cured by doctors such as Hippocrates, formulator of the Hippocratic oath. They would meet the likes of him and also artists and poets, amongst whom was Sophocles, one of the greatest of all the classical dramatists.

With the practice of Nootherapia, art and medicine went hand in glove.

The changing view of what constitutes healthcare finds its support in the classical world, where poets, philosophers and doctors combined to establish good health. With the growing recognition that the state of the mind has its inevitable effect upon the state of the body, the notion of Nootherapia and the important part it has to play is returning to the fore. As far as the ancient Greeks were concerned, changing somebody's state of mind was achieved by bringing them back to their natural state of harmony. They considered that the 'Eros' principle, the power of love, was the most effective way of achieving this.

In Plato's *Symposium*, the physician-philosopher Eryximachos, declares:

Medicine must indeed be able to make the most hostile elements in the body loving and friendly towards one another. It was by means of knowing how to introduce 'Eros' and harmony in these that, as the poets say, and I also believe, our forefather Asklepios established this art of ours.

Eryximachos is stating that, as far as myth is concerned, love was at the centre of the medicine practised in the spirit of Asklepios.

PRACTICE
- Consider your own health. Look to your own state of mind and body.
- Observe what it is in your own way of thinking that creates discord.
- Observe the tensions in the body that are generated by this discord. Let it all go, the physical and the mental. Find harmony of mind and wholeness of body.

When love speaks

The body may be healed directly by material means, but if the cause remains then the effects must necessarily recur. What is called for is a change of mind – Metanoia. Metanoia requires nothing other than the resolving of discord into harmony.

At Epidauros love was introduced in the form of harmony and rhythm in music, dance and poetry (epic, lyric and dramatic), in the form of gymnastic and athletic movement, and, lastly, in artistic creation, in seeking the beauty to be found in architecture, sculpture and painting.

The healers of ancient Greece were certain that the contemplation of the beautiful was a primary factor in the elevation and spiritualization of the human mind, and with this elevation came health, harmony and wealth of every kind. The wealth referred to was of a kind that enriches us at every level when it is freed from the impediments that impoverish our experience of life.

The purpose of this kind of art was to encourage people to free themselves from the subtle constraints confining their thinking. In this respect its function was no different than that of Shakespeare's plays, which express the eternal truths and by so doing elevate and harmonize the human soul. Let us hear once more what Shakespeare says about the poet's relationship with the Venus principle:

> *When love speaks, the voice of all the gods*
> *Make heaven drowsy with the harmony.*
> *Never durst poet touch a pen to write*
> *Until his pen were tem'red with love's sighs:*
> *O, then his lines would ravish savage ears*
> *And plant in tyrants mild humility.*

No age entirely escapes from the activities of savages and tyrants, and sometimes it would seem we are afflicted by an internal tyranny of our own making. The Greeks – like Shakespeare – believed that there existed as an eternal principle, Harmony, and that this manifested in many different ways, and that exposure to the principle, in all its manifestations, is health-giving to both mind and body.

If we were to follow this belief, we would also have to recognize that, for there to be health of mind and body, not only for the individual but for the family and for the nation, Harmony as a principle has to be evoked in the music we make, in the buildings we build, in our poetry and dance, and that the primary function of the arts is to bring about harmony through the elevation of the soul.

PRACTICE
- Practice the art of living. Love life, and do it beautifully.
- Grant the things around you their own beauty.
- Get rid of the clutter. Care for the rest. Let everything shine through the care you give it.
- Above all, love yourself through the way you love others. This is the way to subdue the tyranny of mean-minded emotions.

Elevation of the soul

The phrase 'elevation of the soul' has a grand ring about it, but what does it mean in experience? Before I go on to answer this entirely legitimate question, let's become even more elevated.

In one of the Platonic Dialogues, the *Phaedrus*, this process is beautifully described by Socrates in mythical terms. He speaks of the soul regaining its wings in order to return to those principles that are held in the soul as dimly recognized memories. Our memory of these principles is awakened through the shadows and images perceived by the power of the senses. Socrates says that we make with musical instruments and in song the image of divine harmony, and that the pleasure and satisfaction we feel in the presence of beautiful symmetry is because that form is an image of the perfect ideal of beauty.

That's quite some assertion and certainly requires further explanation, exploration and justification. Within our own experience nobody can deny that there are times when our hearts are lifted by divine music. We can be stunned by the sheer beauty of great architecture. Feelings of this nature are recognized by most of us.

A number of years ago I tried to buy a house. The owner was, like most of us, a mass of contradictions. By the time I met him he was in his late sixties, but when he was younger he had been one of the best known revolutionaries in the country. His life had been dedicated to socialism. Apart from his love for revolution, he had a love of music and architecture. One of his joys was to go off on country walks and stop off at the country churches he came upon.

'Not that I like anything to do with the Church, but I do love the quality of the craftsmanship. It has a beauty.' He was very insistent that I should know this. What he also loved was church music, and he would try his hand whenever he found the organ unlocked in those churches he visited

On one occasion the vicar at one of these churches where he was 'trying his hand', on hearing the organ being played, burst into the church and demanded to know whether he was available to play at the services. 'I'm desperate for an organist!', he said.

Before he knew quite what had happened, this avowed Marxist had agreed to play the organ every Sunday. His love of harmony couldn't be denied, and there he sat playing the organ for the congregation without anyone realizing anything of his revolutionary credentials.

His memory of those principles of which Plato speaks had been aroused and, having been aroused, had to be expressed. He never took down the prized photograph he had of himself shaking hands with Mao. He was quite happy to live with the apparent conflict of ideology.

Regardless of the dogma, he was free enough to respond to that memory and allow conflict to give way to harmony.

PRACTICE

- Whenever the memory arises, respond. Don't allow the constraints we all lay upon ourselves to blot out that memory.
- Give the response time, seek it out even. Listen to music. Go to galleries. Be aware of where you are and what's around you. Allow this awareness to feed your soul and bring mind and body into harmony.

Plucked out of the air

I heard a professional musician tell of her experience of playing the music of Mozart and of how it seemed to her that the music wasn't so much composed as 'plucked out of the air', that somehow he must have been raised up so that he could hear these things. She then went on to describe a dream she had a few days earlier:

I dreamt of a clear blue sky and a yellow cloud moving across it, and there was a finger pointing up. A voice told me to, 'Lift up' and from this meadow I found I did lift up and floated across. After the dream there was a knowledge to be absolutely quiet and still, not turn on the radio, and I sat for a good half hour, and the telephone rang and I was told that my stepmother had died.

If you let consciousness fill you, things become more peaceful and wholesome.

The task of this book is not to discuss the reliability of dreams. What I would like to do is to consider this musician's linked thoughts.

She speaks firstly of the music of Mozart being plucked out of the air. She so evidently feels raised up when she plays his music, for what else would lead her to such a conclusion? Like any deep experience of inspired art, it allows her to visit the place from whence the music first arose, where Mozart was coming from when he first composed it. This is an example of the elevation of the soul we considered earlier.

It was after making her observation about Mozart that she was reminded of the dream and of her experience in the dream of 'lifting up'. She went on to talk about how, having woken from the dream, she was prompted to remain quiet and still. So often when we experience a state of heightened awareness we try to blot it out, by turning on the radio or doing anything but experience something beyond the world in which we feel comfortable, where things are known because we have linked them to our own identity.

Everything about that musician's observation indicates that she had made contact with something beyond what is generally experienced. Remind yourself of her concluding words, which are remarkable for their directness.

If you let consciousness fill you, things become more peaceful and wholesome.

Consciousness cannot be divided. It is by its very nature whole. When there is a lift in our level of consciousness, we become more wholesome, for the divisions disappear, and new knowledge becomes available. At the heart of all this lies peace, the most powerful therapy of all.

PRACTICE
- Give yourself space.
- Seek out the space, and if space should arise don't fill it up with distraction.
- Find peace by filling yourself with the consciousness that is there as a constant behind the movements of the mind, that lies there as love at the heart of all emotion.

Why dash ahead of yourself?

I was walking to work the other day. It was a beautiful day and I wanted to give myself time to take it in. A woman in the same office came beetling past, head down. 'All the time in the world?' she asked as she rushed past. 'And why not?' I thought to myself. 'Why dash ahead of yourself all the time?' I took my time, and I arrived in time. I was 'there' all the time, enjoying the present.

Health is derived from the word 'whole'. Beauty attunes the mind to that whole, for beauty has the sense of wholeness about it. If you look at anything of real beauty it is not 'deconstructed'. It has a sense of its own totality. It doesn't have to dash ahead of itself or prove anything. It has its own completeness and repose.

Let us consider the natural intelligence that governs our bodies. For the body to function harmoniously, it must be free to go about its proper purpose, generating the chemicals that will so perfectly meet its constantly changing needs. If our lives are by nature discordant, racked by tension, if we by education or inclination feed this miraculous mechanism with subtle impressions that generate discord, if we develop patterns of thought that are negative by nature, there will be an inevitable harmful result, not only subtly but also physically. Similarly, if by inclination and education we deliberately change those harmful patterns, that also must have its effect. By being exposed to harmonious sights and sounds, by surrounding ourselves with things that are intrinsically harmonious, by deliberately recognizing the harmony that naturally arises constantly around us, we are automatically giving the principle of harmony within us permission to take on its proper role, and to achieve its proper potency. When our thoughts become harmonious, not only is the mind changed but so also is the body.

PRACTICE

- Find wholeness by being where you are. Don't dash ahead, but instead rest in what's being presented now.
- Find wholeness by connecting.
- When those ideas which encourage disconnection begin to rise in the mind, don't separate yourself out but return to the wholeness.

Fulfilment

Underlying all the thinking we have been exploring in this book is a realm that has its own beauty, the inner harmony of the human spirit. We are exploring ways of gaining access to that world, an access called 'the elevation of the soul', but whether looked on as height or depth, after making our connection we inevitably carry back with us into our experience of daily living a sense of the beauty to be discovered there. From that experience there is the possibility of doing things beautifully, and of giving to our experience of life a general sense of nobility. All of this speaks of wholeness, not fragmentary experience. In a truly healthy mind and body there is continual connection with this wholeness. Our experience of life arises from that sense of wholeness and it is to that sense that we continually refer.

With this sense of wholeness in mind, health in its broadest sense may be defined as being free from physical discomfort and disease, the ability of the mind to think rationally and the heart to be free from negative emotions and to be able to express love. If we accept this definition, health is the expression of our natural state of harmony and happiness. With these two there not only comes a prolongation of life but a greater sense of fulfilment.

When our lives appear narrow and confined, we may ask what is constricting us. The word fulfilment implies two things: a wholeness that can be filled and a willingness to fill that whole. Normally we think of fulfilment being achieved by gaining something. We are the thing that needs to be somehow filled. In the conscious awareness of the Venus Principle we are working from a recognition that we are already filled to the full, and all that is required is to remove those constrictions which prevent us from gaining access to that ever-present fullness.

Our task is not to draw into ourselves something we lack, but to express the fullness that is already there.

PRACTICE

- When you feel those things that divide you off from life, step out of yourself and express the fullness.
- Don't hold back. Give of yourself with enthusiasm, but only so much as the situation demands.
- Don't bombard the situation with all your ideas, but rather serve the situation to the full.

The light of the mind

Although doctors are no longer bound by the Hippocratic Oath, it is still the most fundamental text when it comes to medical ethics. Hippocrates, the most famous of all doctors, makes a very interesting point about medicine. He claims that:

Medicine is related to prophecy, because our ancestor Apollo is the father of both arts.

Apollo, if you recall from the last chapter, was the sun god to the Greeks. He was also the father of the same Asklepios of whom we've already heard. Apollo is best known for being the patron of prophecy, music, poetry and the healing arts. Again you can see how classical thinking intimately links health of mind and body with the inspiration art can provide.

But where does prophecy come in? Prophecy is concerned with the law of cause and effect. A prophet knows that the modes of thinking we adopt now will have their inevitable results in the future. Therefore, when dealing with our negative tendencies, he will endeavour to heal by bringing measure to our minds through the application of reason, and fullness to our hearts through the power of love.

It is little wonder that Apollo was identified with the sun, for the sun has always been held as the physical manifestation of the light of consciousness.

For Shelley, like so many poets before him, Apollo was 'the eye with which the universe beholds itself.' Here he is translating Homer:

> *I am the eye with which the Universe*
> *Beholds itself and knows itself divine;*
> *All harmony of instrument or verse,*
>
> *All prophecy, all medicine is mine,*
> *All light of art or nature; – to my song*
> *Victory and praise in their own right belong*

PRACTICE

- Be aware of light: the light of the sun that bathes us continually, the light of the moon, the light of the stars, fire light, the light of a candle.
- When there is no light, when there is complete darkness or when you close your eyes, be aware of the light of the mind. Connect with the Apollo within.

Be heliotropic

In human terms, what allows the eye to see is our own consciousness. It wasn't for nothing that Apollo was both the god of the sun and of harmony. That light is the source of harmony. As has already been stated, there is no such thing as a divided consciousness, and arising out of that unity is the principle of harmony, the principle that allows us to appreciate unity in diversity. It is this same wholeness that in turn grants health to mind and body.

The philosopher-physician Ficino constantly stated that we must be heliotropic, ever turning towards the sun. In a letter in which he answers a question about why he combines the study of medicine with music, he replies that they both come from Apollo. Apollo, by his vital rays, bestows health and life on all and drives away disease. The music flowing out from the light of reason manifests in voice and instrument, and then from these sounds arise dance and gymnastics.

Thus we may see that music of the soul is led by steps to all the limbs of the body. It is this music that orators, poets, painters, sculptors and architects seek to imitate in their work. Given that there is such strong communion between the music of the soul and of the body, is it surprising that both the body and the soul may be set in order by the same man?

Just as shadows make the sun more obvious, so the discords in music are employed to make the harmonic resolution more potent. The deliberate breaking of proportion in architecture, the interruption of measure and rhythm is likewise designed to create a tension that can be resolved and brought back into repose, thereby bringing to the mind an appreciation of the underlying harmony of proportion. What is true of music and architecture is true of all the arts. But if discord becomes discord for its own sake, tension and all that follows from it must become our predominant experience.

Those soul psychologists of the Renaissance were part of the classical tradition which has formed the backbone of Western civilization. They spoke of the negative faces of Saturn and Mars that created melancholy, malignancy, bad temper and anger. They spoke of how these negative forces needed to be cured by food for the soul so that the soul might be revived, refreshed, recover its faculties and grow whole. Above all, they claimed that Phoebus Apollo, the light of consciousness, was able to provide that food.

Phoebus alone brings peace to the soul, and of you will my soul ever sing.

PRACTICE

- In those times when the shadows of suffering are thrown across your life, be heliotropic – turn towards the light of your own consciousness, that which remains untouched by anything it illuminates, light or dark, and that alone brings harmony and peace. The pain will inevitably remain, but it will be tempered by something else. This is the beauty that heals. It is the light of love.

Chapter seven

The emotional ground

IN THE PRACTICAL DEVELOPMENT of our understanding of the nature of love, we are by necessity connecting with our hearts. We are learning how the heart functions and the extent of its influence. We are discovering how to encourage creative emotion and transcend the constraints of negative thoughts, not by suppressing them – which is nothing more than adding further constraints – but by going beyond their expression to what lies at the heart of the emotional realm. In so doing we are connecting with the most fundamental of all emotions. Regardless of our immediate experience, in our heart of hearts lies love.

There are so many expressions associated with the heart: warm, cold, soft, hard, faint, big, cruel, heavy, light, sacred. We talk about taking heart and losing heart, being out of heart and even eating our heart out. Judging by all this the heart is a pretty active instrument that doesn't confine itself to merely pumping blood round the body.

We think we know where it is located, having our heart in the right place, but even there we cannot be too certain. At times it is in our boots and at other times it is in our mouths. This is when it is fully functioning, but there are occasions when the heart aches and is even broken.

It may be claimed that the heart rules us far more completely than anything else. Even those who pride themselves on being cool headed and clear minded may achieve this by becoming cold hearted, and thereby in a contradictory way be more firmly ruled by the heart than those who appear to give way to their emotions.

So what is this emotional centre of our being and how might we escape from what often appears to be its tyranny? How might we discover its true nature, and how might emotion and reason – heart and head – find a fulfilling relationship that will allow us to grow as human beings? What lies at the true centre of our being, and how might we connect with and employ what is to be found in our heart of hearts?

PRACTICE

- Notice the kinds of emotions you are susceptible to. You might even give them a name.
- Rather than totally identifying with them, get to know them as you would people in a play. In this way they won't be *the real you* so much as characters who make their own entrances and exits.

Ghosts in the machine

So here they are, these players on the stage of life. All of them come and go, stimulated by outside events. Sometimes they are in total opposition to one another, and yet whilst they hold the stage we find them totally convincing. We are them and they are us. These are the real ghosts in the machine, if ghosts can be called real. When we look back and consider the characters to which we have lent our identity, they are legion. They may come in a moment of madness and lead us into the most insane antics, although at the time appearing entirely plausible. Some of these performers are so popular they are always on stage, booked for life. They have almost taken us over.

That is as it is, and we must gain some comfort from the fact that everybody else is in the same situation. These characters activate us. They pop out of the situations we face: the angry man behind the wheel, the indignant customer with goods that don't quite match his desires, the glamorous hostess with nothing to wear, the commanding presence and the born loser, the petty dictator and the great down-trodden, the utterly certain and the totally unsure, and more and yet more. They are indeed legion, and it is possible to play them all without noticing where one ends and the next begins. Why? Because we totally identify with every one of them.

Play them often enough and they never leave, and every time we meet a situation from their point of view, seeing things as if through their eyes, their presence becomes reinforced. Each of these characters has a strong emotional quality that becomes engrained. And it doesn't stop at the individual. We are all susceptible to family influences, and it goes without saying that, in addition to our individual oddities, there are such things as national characteristics. We hold something in common with our fellow countrymen, and we are proud of those characteristics: proud of being oddly English, peculiarly French, extravagantly American or idiosyncratically Dutch. And there is also the tenor of the times to take into account.

As has already been said, this is as it is, and in a way we shouldn't be overly concerned, much better to be amused. The last thing we are seeking in this book is some kind of make over, cultivating our better points and toning down the worst. In making the Venus Principle a key factor in the way we conduct our lives, we won't have to tinker with externals. Indeed, if we were to do so it would only lead to us cultivating another cast of stock characters.

We shouldn't be worried about our nature – that would be looking in the wrong direction. Change, if it is to take place, comes by revelation rather than manipulation. Change takes place in our heart of hearts by making contact with the underlying substratum of our emotions. It takes place by not being propelled into outward reaction by petty irritation and anxiety, but by referring within, to that which is constant and true. By making this our reference, there will be an effect, and those oddities of ours, which might once have been the impediments to free and natural relationships, become the very things that give us our own peculiar appeal. They become the vehicles for the expression of love. What else might we express when we really speak and act from the heart?

PRACTICE

- The next time you feel like reacting blindly to some attack on what you hold dear about yourself, pause before making a response, stay at the point of stillness and love from which all movement arises. See what is there, and then – without claiming it as your own possession – find what really meets the situation, creatively not reactively.

Human legacy

The word 'emotions' gives a clear indication of their fundamental nature. They move. They are in motion. Some of the emotions we entertain can be extremely violent. Some of them are unrelenting, holding us in their grip for years. In some cultures they are handed down from generation to generation. They can become a legacy of hate.

Fortunately for most of us, this won't be our legacy. If you are in any doubt about the power of negative emotion even on the most mild mind, try succumbing to it and then observe its effect on those around you and also on yourself. It exhausts us, or it burns us up, or it gnaws away at us. What it doesn't do is to nourish us, nor does it grant happiness or freedom or understanding.

If our intent is to develop as human beings, we can't afford to give way to negative emotion, and the best way to overcome negative emotion is to develop the capacity to love. One of love's most noticeable features is the power of forgiveness, both for those who might have been the cause of our negative feelings and ourselves in giving way to them. Nothing is more damaging than self-recrimination and self-criticism. Nothing discourages our development more than belittling ourselves. Therefore, self-forgiveness is crucial.

All our desires emerge from the source of love, for in pursuing our desires we are pursuing our happiness. The wise constantly repeat that the source of our happiness is love. If it is allowed to function naturally, this process will work for our evolution as human beings. If we lack discrimination, however, it may serve a more destructive purpose. How we seek our happiness is dependent on our level of understanding. The greater our understanding, the clearer will be our appreciation of those factors in our lives which will grant lasting happiness. If we follow the principle of love, there must be growth, but if we serve anything but, there must be decay. There are no half measures in this. There must be either expansion or contraction. In nature nothing remains the same. Seek, therefore, the constant that lies behind this constant change of emotion.

Love is a constant and the more there is access to it, the more chance there is of human development, for it is love that makes humanity humane. Love grants true appreciation and satisfaction. Love is one of the central and most profound of all human legacies.

PRACTICE

- Consider yourself and your own development as a human being. When in your life did you gain more happiness and understanding? What were you in touch with that made all the difference?
- Think of those around you, the people you know. Think of those whose judgement you value. Think of those in whom you would be happy to confide, confident that they would listen with understanding and sympathy. What ingredient do these people possess?
- Having identified that ingredient, adopt it yourself, and then return to it over and over again, as many times as you can

remember. Make that ingredient your source of action.

- Don't be swayed by passing passions, but rest instead in the most profound of all passions, the constant to which Shakespeare refers to in the sonnets: 'that looks on tempests and is never shaken beneath constant change', the principle of love.

So what's at the root of my frustrations?

Let us try to map our way through the storm of emotion as it batters us back and forth, rippling around us. Of what does it consist and what's at the centre of it all?

I was told an amusing story the other day, by a man who is in business with his brother. They were due to attend a meeting at the premises of a company with which they hoped to do business. Unfortunately, they had become caught up in traffic. The time of their meeting was getting closer, and his brother was becoming more and more frustrated. Then, to make matters worse, his brother realized that he had forgotten to take the relevant details, which included the address and phone number of the company. Needless to say, his anger and frustration mounted to the point where he insisted on driving backwards and forwards, round and round the streets of this town, of which he had only a passing knowledge, in a desperate attempt to find the place.

In the end the man seized the wheel from his brother and ordered him to pull over. He told him to drop the whole thing, to come to rest instead of being driven by his anger and frustration. Remarkably, his brother stopped the car and attempted to do as he was advised. Once he had achieved some freedom from his agitations, he was amazed to discover that not only did he remember the address, but that they were parked a hundred yards from the place they had been so desperately seeking.

This is a classic case of what was described as his brother 'coming to his senses', literally, and of how he had previously been 'driven out of his mind' by the emotion that had taken hold of him.

This is our mind, but there are times when we become somehow separated from it, inevitably disconnected from our senses, from our hearing, our seeing and, more importantly, from our intelligence. It's little wonder that in this process we lose our direction. Notice, too, how in the way we talk about these things there is innate understanding of the process, maybe because we find ourselves in this predicament so often. This was certainly the case in the example given. Situations like that had happened to the man's brother over and over again.

And who was at the centre of it all, for him, for all of us? An idea we have about ourselves: all our hopes and fears, all our attachments. What else could it possibly be about? Yet the very thing that we hold most dear has the power to drive us from ourselves, debilitate us and reduce our level of awareness to that of someone possessed. What is more, we go on repeating the same behaviour over and over again, often failing to learn the most obvious lessons. Why? Because of our total attachment to those things which generate our joys and our frustrations.

In the following four lines the poet William Blake describes an altogether different approach:

> *He who binds to himself a joy*
> *Doth the winged life destroy,*
> *But he who kisses life as it flies*
> *Lives in eternity's sunrise.*

Or, to put it even more simply:

Claim nothing. Enjoy.

This is how to free ourselves from the bonds of anger and frustration, for things sought for and lost. It is also the way to free ourselves from the destructive power of negative emotion, because it opens up the principle of love.

PRACTICE

- When joys come our way, enjoy them to the full but don't hang on. Let them go. Let them be as they are. Don't try to milk something more from them which we hope might add in some way to our stock of happiness.
- All things have their measure except the eternal principles, which are constant and forever new. This is why Blake says that, when we come to understand this and it becomes part of our immediate experience, we live in 'eternity's sunrise'.
- This is the place where we might discover real and lasting happiness. It is not somewhere beyond the far horizon. It is immediately to hand, here and now. Remember the words: 'Claim nothing. Enjoy.'
- The same applies to the frustrations as well as the joys. Do the same. Let them go. There's nothing to lose in this and so much to gain.

Common ground

We have our relationships. Friends swim into our lives. Many drift away. When we meet again, perhaps after years, it's hard to believe that years have passed; so much has been shared, there is a sense of common ground which is impervious to time. This common ground may be accounted for as nothing more than shared experience, but there's a sense of something else besides. It is the emotional setting in which the relationship is shared. We call it friendship, and we value it greatly. Friendship is not only to do with those with whom we share friendship, but also to do with what is discovered in ourselves by means of friendship.

What is discovered in friendship is 'the common ground'. It is 'the common ground' that unites people and forges relationships. The term 'common ground' seems to suggest a place where people meet and discover things about each other which they hold in common: understanding, emotion, common interests, ideas and general outlook. This seems to be the case, but is that all, or yet again is there something more, something lying beyond the things you can point to?

The 'common ground' may seem to be something that arises out of the relationship, but when two people discover 'common ground', it may be more to do with what is brought to light in the place where they meet rather than a sharing of what is brought to that place. When a genuine meeting takes place, the place is the constant factor, whilst those who share the relationship come and go, returning perhaps after many years. What in truth is discovered in this place is that such a place exists.

This place has been there all along. If we are fortunate, we visit it regularly. It is easy to point to our friends and think that the place is 'over there', to be found in them. They may provide the means of entering this place, but in reality we have always been in possession of it. It is an underlying constant, and, naturally enough, the more access we have to it the more friends we attract, because everybody wants to open the gate to that place themselves.

Having opened the gate and explored that place in its fullness, relationships become easy and simple. Mother, son, father, sister, brother, friends – all relationships may reveal some aspect of love. We need only to respond naturally to these relationships. Simple and truthful relationships are all we need to maintain.

Complications arise only when we take something that is to be found in the 'common ground' and lay upon it some personal claim. In all relationships we must seek to return to the source.

This source is what lies at the heart of all our emotions: the principle of love. Only when we refuse to recognize the source and identify ourselves with the objects of our love and try to claim them for ourselves does everything start to go wrong. Go to the place where all our desires arise. If we return there, our friendships will quite naturally deepen of their own accord and more and more of the common ground will be discovered.

'Common ground' is the source of all true emotion. Only when we fail to recognize its presence or forget what we once knew, identifying with the relationship which allowed us to enter there, seeking something in that relationship for ourselves, do things go wrong. We must return to the 'common ground', by turning in and allowing our relationships to find their fullness and fruition in that place from which they arose, the emotional ground of love.

PRACTICE

- In your friendships recognize not only the value of those with whom you share your friendships, but also recognize the context within which they manifest.
- Turn to yourself and share with your friends what is to be found there in the common ground of love.

The garden of love

In medieval poetry, the garden of love was a commonplace. It appeared over and over again in poetry.

> *This garden full of leaves and flowers*
> *And craft of man's hands so curiously*
> *Arrayed had this garden, truly*
> *That never was there garden of prize*
> *But if it were the very Paradise.*
> *The odour of the flowers and the fresh sight*
> *Would have made any heart to light.*

This is Chaucer providing a suitable setting for love, a beautiful garden in May, a beautiful time of the year – the trees in new leaf, the vitality of nature in all her vigour. Sometimes that new green attacks our senses with its vibrancy. You cannot help but be conscious of the new life surging forth after the dormancy of winter. Green is the symbolic colour of regeneration. In Christian iconography it is the colour of hope, of resurrection. The sap no longer sinks towards the earth but rises instead towards the light. No wonder the green of May reflects that light so brilliantly.

Green expresses the love of light and of life, and it is no great wonder that the greatest of all Greek sculptors, Phidias, carved a green Venus. Go into any of our great parks. See what it's like on a sunlit afternoon in May and you will find that the medieval garden of love is not that far from our experience.

This is why people love gardening. There is something utterly essential about turning the earth, encouraging things to grow. There is a service being offered. The whole thing is dedicated to the principle of beauty. Nobody takes an uncultivated piece of land in the thought of making a garden without a desire to create something of beauty in that place. And the whole thing has its magic. To take dry seeds in the palm of your hand and then witness these pieces of dust flower and fruit is to enter into the mysterious process of creation. Those who love their gardens are intimately aware of this process. They become part of it.

I was in my garden planting vegetables over the weekend. It was a perfect morning for gardening. The sun was shining and yet there was a breeze to keep things cool. The soil had been well prepared. Everything was right for growing. When I had finished, I thought back on all the years that I'd done the same kind of thing. There was something about caring for that small plot of land that went beyond having fresh vegetables to eat. It was part of a deeper relationship. It was as if I had been feeding the place, and the place in turn had been feeding me. We had entered into an entirely satisfying relationship.

To find common ground with a piece of earth is indeed an entirely satisfying thing. Being fed by it involves much more than having fresh vegetables for the table. Something within is also being fed in the process.

PRACTICE

- Look at the natural world. Be aware of what is being fed by connection with that world. By opening the senses wide to what nature provides, let the heart be restored.

- There is such a thing as the love of life. Why put up with a dull heart and mind when you may allow the vitality of nature to assault the senses?

When nothing undone remains

It was a perfect day
For sowing; just
As sweet and dry was the ground
As tobacco-dust.

I tasted deep the hour
Between the far
Owl's chuckling first soft cry
And the first star.

A long stretched hour it was;
Nothing undone
Remained; the early seeds
All safely sown.

And now, hark at the rain,
Windless and light,
Half a kiss, half a tear,
Saying goodnight.

EDWARD THOMAS, *Sowing*

Sowing seeds in the ground offers its own satisfaction. Sowing seeds in soil perfect for germination gives an even greater satisfaction. When after sowing there comes the rain, that gives both a sense of satisfaction and of blessed completion.

Of course, there never can be completion, not as far as nature is concerned, for the one certainty about nature is that it's forever undergoing change. Why else would we plant seeds if we didn't hope for change, for the whole process of germination, growth and fruition? Even that is not the end. The cycle of the seasons turns in constant rotation. Despite this knowledge, we naturally seek some satisfying conclusion, an action brought to rest.

We live in this imaginary realm called time. We know it passes, because we look back with the aid of memory into the past, and we project the images formed in the mind into the imagined future. In our mind's eye the seeds we have planted sprout and green leaves rise spiralling towards the sun. We see them grow until the time comes again for fruition.

This is all part of the changing course of nature, and any attempt to find completion here is bound to be frustrated. True completion and complete satisfaction will not be discovered after some imagined period of time. The only time when it can possibly be discovered is now. The present grants its own completion, its own satisfaction. Step free from the onward rush of events and enter the fullness of the present.

PRACTICE
- Make each moment its own completion by entering more fully into that moment.
- When Edward Thomas gained his satisfaction, 'when nothing undone remained', it was at no other time but the moment. The present is its own beginning and end.

Finding rest in your own presence

Often what is left undone in a task has nothing to do with its physical aspect, but more to do with the inner connection, the inner rest and contentment discovered in the deed itself.

In Edward Thomas's poem there is an evident sense of the inner contentment that comes with the ability to rest in the present. So often we skid across the surface of experience and in the process fail to meet what is really there.

At any moment, even when performing the simplest of tasks, there is to be discovered the source of true satisfaction, if only we allow ourselves time to rest in the present and to refer the experience inwardly. If we were to take this up as a conscious practice, this would undoubtedly grant true satisfaction. When we breathlessly dash on to the next thing, we fail to taste what is really before us. We fail to savour the moment.

All this has its effect upon our emotional ground. To connect fully with each moment, in whatever way the moment has of presenting itself, is the only way genuinely to care for what lies on the surface of life and, at the same time, what lies within, the emotional ground of our own being.

It is the dictates of desire that make us continually race on to the next thing and in the process subconsciously downgrade most of what comes our way, believing the thing we desire, the thing we lack, to be the important thing.

When desire is present there must be a sense of lack. We don't desire the things we already possess, and therefore we chase ahead of ourselves and fail to value the one thing that's of vital importance, for us the only thing we truly possess: what life is presenting now. By referring things inwardly, we make full connection with that. We allow for a full and proper completion and, with it, true satisfaction and a deeper experience of life. Whilst we are driven, in whatever way, there can be no real satisfaction, nor rest.

In the act of referring things inwardly, we are not only finding real rest in the moment, we are also in the process tending what is fundamental to us, the inner ground of our emotional being. If we could transcend all those agitations that seem to deprive us of our rest and satisfaction, we would find that lying there all the time is the very thing we hope to gain from all this outer activity – proper completion and full happiness. By tending the inner ground we would truly transform our experience of life.

To live a life on the physical plain only is to miss the point of it all. There is the surface of life, and there is life's inner being. If the outer surface appears to be all activity, its inner nature is stillness and rest, the source of true satisfaction. Therefore, if happiness is our aim, we must tend the inner ground.

PRACTICE

- When you feel you are being driven by events, remember that you are the one behind the wheel. Take your foot off the accelerator. Make full contact with whatever it is you are engaged in.
- Get in touch with those around you. Give them your time. Allow them to find rest in your presence and in the process allow yourself to find rest in your own presence.

Love of the land

My father had a vision. I could never understand it when I was younger, but now I'm beginning to understand. We are New Zealanders and my father is a geographer. He has a strong feeling for the land. And he had it in mind for quite a time to purchase some property north of Auckland, where my family live. He wanted some land to care for in accordance with this vision of his. It was a desire that remained as a dream until the time arose when there appeared, seemingly by chance, the possibility of buying a run down farm of 300 acres in just the sort of area he had in mind.

Since buying the farm, he has spent his time developing it. Some of what he does involves restoring the land, but in addition he has planted trees that will not come to maturity until after his death. There is an ideal that he holds constantly in mind, and everything he does is dictated by that ideal. This ideal is directly related to his love of the land. The sense is that whatever he is pursuing will not be achieved in his own life time, although he will pursue it for as long as he is able, nor is it limited to any desire he has for himself. He works out of a sense of devotion to something much larger than any individual.

Desires of the sort spoken of in this observation possess greater nobility than is usual. They arise 'out of a devotion to something much larger than any individual'. In this case the devotion is to do with an ideal associated with land.

From the way his son speaks, we get an idea of what that ideal might be. It's to do with true husbandry, the belief that we should give back to the land more than we take from it. This doesn't just mean caring for the soil, although that must have a key part to play in it all. It's also to do with bringing that land to its proper fullness and fruition, a place that feeds at every level. To do this, an understanding of the nature of the place must be gained, and that means working with it rather than forcing an individual desire upon it.

When we talk about people having a feeling for the land, it means love, a genuine care, a desire that this particular place with which they are associated should find its proper expression. How do they know it's to be found there? Because the same thing exists in their own hearts. There could be no recognition if this were not so. They are tending the outer in accordance with a deep emotional insight, and because of this insight it's the inner they are tending as well.

This is the nature of true idealism, for although it requires considerable individual input – that's clear from the observation – it goes far beyond any personal claim.

The father has planted trees that will not come to fruition till after his death. This is what gives him the energy, and it's what will make his endeavour of lasting value. He is planting those trees for the love of it.

PRACTICE
- Whatever you do, do it for the love it.
- If you feel that love has gone out of what you are doing, come to rest in your own inner ground, where all true ideals are to be found. Work from there.

Something will always remain

There's a particular spot on a hillside overlooking the Wye Valley. It's part of my childhood. I strongly associate myself with that place. I went back there quite recently whilst visiting my parents. Nothing had changed. I still felt the same feelings. I have invested something of my own identity in that place, yet the thought came to mind: 'This was here long before I was born and will be here long after I am dead. So what's so personal about it?' Strangely enough the thought didn't in any way diminish my personal feelings, rather deepened them. It was as if something in me was part of something that would always remain, regardless of who was there to experience it.

What is being described is a moment of understanding. These are powerful moments and will remain as formative influences. The place described, this spot overlooking the Wye Valley, was important to the man as a child, something with which he strongly associated. When he returned there as an adult, it was to discover something more, or more likely to formulate what he already knew.

It would seem that the discovery he made had something to do both with the place and what was within him. He seemed to touch on that abiding presence which we all possess, which, though transcendent of our individual life, when accessed allows us a greater depth in our experience of life. Not only that, it also grants a greater significance to anything we lend ourselves to in our lives. We do things more beautifully, with greater energy, care and intelligence when this presence finds its expression. Why? Because it encourages us to love what we are doing.

PRACTICE

- Feed the inner ground by referring things inwardly. Learn to live reflectively.
- Consider the significance of what you do and what you give expression to.
- By cultivating the emotional ground, what you bring to fruition will allow others to recognize the existence of that presence in themselves.

The image of ourselves

Botticelli was an artist whose aim was to express these divine principles within. This book is named after one his paintings, *The Birth of Venus*, but there is another of Botticelli's paintings, *The Birth of Spring*, which is even better known. It is set in a garden of love, presided over by Venus. This painting is constantly reproduced in a hundred different ways. It seems there's hardly a surface that can take a colour print upon which it hasn't appeared. Yet despite it being so familiar an image, somehow it retains its original freshness.

It portrays life arising from dormant winter, once more clothed with colour. The spirit of life returns. In the sacred grove depicted the three Graces dance in their perpetual round. Venus governs the movement of creation arising from the creative principle, turning in a circle of manifestation back to whence it came. On the edge of the grove the figure of Mercury stirs the clouds with his magic wand, his Caduceus, turning his face to what lies beyond the beauty of this physical world, back to the soul of the world.

Ficino, who did so much to encourage the soul-making philosophy that had such an impact on Renaissance thinking and Renaissance art, wrote a letter which contains ideas that scholars believe profoundly influenced the conception of Botticelli's painting. Ficino describes Venus as central to human nature.

Nothing great can be possessed by us on earth, unless we men can be taken by no other bait whatsoever than our own nature. Beware that you never despise her, perhaps thinking that human nature is born of earth, for human nature herself is a nymph with body surpassing ... For indeed her soul and spirit are love and kinship; her eyes are majesty and magnanimity; her hands are liberality and greatness in action; her feet gentleness and restraint. Finally her whole is harmony and integrity, honour and radiance.

What is it about the *The Birth of Spring* that elicits such a powerful response? Has it a mystery lying beneath its seductive surface? Is it speaking to us of something that is much closer to us than we might imagine? Does it evoke the powers within our souls?

There is no doubt that the painting is meant to conjure up in the minds of all those who see it an image of Venus herself, not only as an object of beauty but as a reminder of our own 'majesty and magnanimity, gentleness and restraint', our own 'harmony, integrity, honour and radiance'. These are the divine spirits that live within. This is what lies in our heart of hearts. No wonder there remains such a ready response to this powerful picture of love. In Ficino's estimation it reminds us of ourselves.

PRACTICE

- By referring things inwardly, the beauty that arises before our senses will connect us with the beauty within.
- Botticelli's painting of Venus was conceived as a magic talisman whose beauty would awaken the principle of love. Many who have seen her will recognize what is being spoken of here. But you don't have to go to the Uffizi Gallery in Florence. You may recognize the principle of love anywhere.
- Look for the beauty that lies before you, then take it home to the sacred grove of your own heart. This is the emotional ground we all possess, and, like any piece of property, it needs tending.

Chapter eight

Landscape of the soul

ONE OF THE GREAT THINGS about the world is that it is not short of beauty. On a news broadcast one night was a recording of an astronaut on a space walk tenuously attached to his space craft high above the earth's surface. Whilst desperately trying to connect up huge pieces of equipment, struggling to achieve his difficult task in the most perilous of situations, he suddenly looked down and realized that he was passing over Italy. He cried out in wonder to the other astronauts: 'Look, Italy! Isn't it beautiful!'

No, there is no shortage of beauty, but it can only be discovered when we become aware of its presence, and only fully appreciated when it is taken within. Then, not only do we discover the beauty without, but we also tend the emotional ground of our own hearts by discovering that same beauty is to be discovered there in its fullness. This is the fundamental truth we have been stressing.

In a world of urgency, when so much of our time is devoted to results, the inherent beauty of things – our own inherent beauty – is easily forgotten.

W. H. Davies concludes his poem *Leisure* with these lines:

> *No time to turn at Beauty's glance,*
> *And watch her feet, how they can dance.*
>
> *No time to wait till her mouth can*
> *Enrich that smile her eyes began*
>
> *A poor life this is if, full of care,*
> *We have no time to stand and stare*

There is no time to stand and stare whilst struggling with the space programme, but beauty can strike us unawares all in an instant, no matter when or where. But these are exceptional circumstances we are talking about. I suspect that one is pretty well wide awake whilst dangling off a satellite, open to beauty. There is no doubt that the more conscious we are, the more we are aware of beauty, but, unless the circumstances are exceptional, we have to cultivate beauty by giving her time.

Cézanne was asked why he painted the same scene over and over again. He replied that he wanted to enter ever more deeply into it; the connection was the real thing, the painting but the product. This is giving beauty time, and in the process tending the inner landscape, the landscape of the soul.

PRACTICE

- Find real quality of life by giving yourself time. Come into the moment.
- Connect with colour and form, light and space.
- Let go of emotional confines, and touch the underlying stillness.

The presence of light and love

Speaking of Cézanne, here are his very words:

Personally I'd like to lose myself in nature, grow again with nature, like nature have the stubborn shades of the rocks, the rational obstinacy of the mountain, the fluidity of the air, and the warmth of the sun. In a green my whole brain would flow with the sap rising through a tree's veins. Out in front of us there is a great presence of light and love, the hovering universe, the tentativeness of things.

Such a clear expression of intent indicates the depth of his vision. From the physical, his mind penetrates and connects with the subtle qualities: obstinacy, fluidity, warmth; vitality is recognized in the green of organic life and the flow of sap rising, but even then he goes beyond to the great presence of light and love, the hovering universe, the tentativeness of things. Here, so obviously speaking from his own experience, Cézanne gives us a vision of the artist connecting with the soul of nature, approaching the quantum world of potentiality from whence everything arises.

As has been repeated often in this book, one of the most important and immediate ways for most of us to recognize these underlying principles comes through our appreciation of beauty. Constable, whose calm evocation of the beauty of English landscape has made him one of the best loved of painters, writes this to his wife of his own appreciation:

Nothing can exceed the beauty of the country at this time. its freshness – its amenity – the very breeze that passes the window is delightful. It has the voice of nature.

I believe we can do nothing worse than indulge in useless sensibility – but I can hardly tell you what I feel at the sight from the window where I am now writing of the fields in which I have so often walked. A beautiful, calm, Autumnal setting sun glowing upon the garden of the Rectory and adjacent fields.

There is room enough for natural painting. The great vice of the present day is bravura, an attempt at something beyond truth … Fashion always had, and will have its day – but Truth [in all things] only will last and can have just claims on posterity.

In these words from the soul, Constable expresses his deep devotion to the beauty of the natural world that lies before him, a beauty that he so perfectly captures in his own paintings. His feelings also naturally take him on to express his devotion to Truth, which, as he rightly says, is not subject to passing fashion. Truth by its very nature is always true. When the artist becomes devoted to truth he searches for its presence in all that he sees and then seeks to express it in his work. This kind of devotion is no different than that shown by the great scientists, many of whom desire the same thing. They wish to approach, in Max Planck's words, 'the ultimate mystery of being', the truth itself.

Inspired by this desire, the philosophers, artists and poets are led to explore this landscape of the soul and bring back the record of their explorations so that all may recognize that such a place exists.

PRACTICE

- The vision of geniuses may seem far from our own experience, but why dismiss the possibility? Take Cézanne's approach and look for the inner qualities of things.
- We all recognize them, sharply responding when we are barely aware of their presence. Bring them into view.
- Consciously come to recognize what those qualities are in the people and situations we meet.
- Begin to see life as the play of these qualities, and then go on to recognize the underlying 'presence of light and love' in which they manifest.

Were the eye not of the sun

Cézanne and Constable are people who used their eyes. They looked and then looked again, but their looking didn't stop at the exterior nature of things. They went beyond the surface and captured the inner spirit. It's this power that makes them great artists. This is why we value them so highly. They have developed the capacity for insight, and we, in our recognition of the beauty of their work, are developing it too. They are our teachers.

Goethe made this interesting observation about our eyes:

> Were the eye not of the sun,
> How could we behold the light?
> If God's might and ours were not as one,
> How could His work enchant our sight?

Goethe emphasized the significance of 'Bildung', or self-transformation, in his thinking. He saw the human being as constantly engaged in a process of self-formation. He talks of light giving rise to the organ of perception which allowed light to be recognized.

The eye may be said to owe its existence to light, which calls forth, as it were, a sense that is like itself; the eye, in short, is formed in reference to light; the inner light corresponding to the light without.

Birds who have somehow got trapped in underground caves, lacking light, lose their sight. For eyes to form, we need light.

Goethe talks about how this applies to the organs of sense and also to those organs of the mind that allow us intuitive insight. He claimed that, if the possibility of insight is discounted in our thinking, there is no way that the organs of intuition will develop within us. He believed that the purpose of art is to draw the mind to the eternal principles and in the process help develop the organs of insight that might appreciate those principles.

When analysis was done on Einstein's brain it was discovered that a certain part of it was 15 per cent larger than the average brain. This, however, was not so unexpected. The expansion of his brain was in that area associated with mathematical manipulation. Violinists have enlarged brains in the area connected with the manipulation of the hands. The body, as one might imagine, is entirely responsive to the use that is made of it. Regardless of what the mind picks up or lays aside, the body will naturally follow. When we speak of people being open-minded or big-hearted perhaps we are not speaking in entirely metaphorical terms. Perhaps we can develop not only the subtle organs of insight and compassion but also their associated physical organs.

PRACTICE

- Develop the capacity for insight by opening the heart and mind and looking again and again.
- Connect the mind with the senses. Look at what lies before you – really look.
- See what is presented on the surface and then look beyond. Practice this in all situations. Practice this particularly in your relationships.

The herald of inward and eternal beauty

Remember how we said that the paintings for which Botticelli is still revered had more than a decorative purpose, that they were designed to arouse memory, that they were painted in the belief that the soul is capable of not only looking out into the material world, which by its very nature is full of things that must come to pass, but is also able to look within, into the realm of the 'Beautiful and the Good'?

This is how Emerson, the New England philosopher, described the relationship between the inner and outer worlds:

The last or highest expression of the final cause of Nature was nothing other than to act as the herald of inward and eternal beauty.

We have the works of inspired men and women to arouse our memory, but we also have the beauty of the world before us. Instead of this world being a continual source of distraction, a multitude of involvements, treat it instead as 'the herald of inward and eternal beauty'.

PRACTICE

- Let go of all those concerns that habitually capture the mind.
- See in what is immediately before you something of the eternal beauty of things.
- Use your senses to connect with the world around you. Enjoy all that's to be discovered there. Recognize it as 'the herald of inward and eternal beauty'.
- Take time to appreciate everything that is encountered, first outwardly and then inwardly.

Where does the soul end?

We're so used to thinking of things being broken down and separated out that it is hard to think of things in their totality, all levels interacting, everything behaving appropriately according to that level. Things subtle do have their physical effect, and things physical have their subtle influence. Sometimes it is hard to decide where one ends and the other begins. Here, for instance, is an observation describing a situation that must accord with our own experience.

In the light of the discussion we had been having the previous week, I got my secretary some flowers, and then we both considered how to make the office look better. It wasn't me being nice to my secretary. We both really looked at the office's needs, and I will buy some more. You start by focussing on good things and it spreads. Being in the moment is more enjoyable and is not contrived.

Flowers in the office not only change the physical environment but also the subtle, and in changing our subtle environment we are physically reconstituting our bodies. The whole thing is interactive.

Much has been written about stress and its physical effects. When under stress the body does act appropriately at its level. Its response is lawful, as indeed are the stress-related illnesses that may follow from long exposure to stressful situations. Stress is a subtle matter, but its results may be far from subtle. Stress affects the mind, but upon the instant, mind stuff is materialized in the body.

We have considered the principles of harmony and their effect upon mind and body. It is not the purpose of this book to produce antidotes to stress, but inevitably if these divine principles are consciously acknowledged and deliberately evoked, then stress which afflicts us most when we are at our most fearful and isolated must inevitably dissolve as the greater unity is more greatly appreciated.

In addition, we may serve that greater unity. In the case cited above it was simply a matter of appreciating what the office needed and consciously serving that need. But it goes beyond that.

Notice what was said about good things. They spread. Just as we may make a fraught situation worse by entering into the spirit of tension and conflict, and thereby generating yet more of the same, so by serving the greater need, no matter how it might manifest, love's influence must have its effect. In addition, by remembering that things physical have their subtle dimension, attending to the physical in the right spirit will harmonize the subtle environment, free up the subtle world and create new possibility. Flowers in the office makes economic sense if they are put there in the right spirit.

And when do we as individuals make a start with this new approach to the balance sheet?

Being in the moment is more enjoyable and is not contrived.

His final comment, which may on the face of things seem somewhat out of context, has its point, because it gives a very clear indication of the only time for this kind of work. Now. It also gives an indication of what results from that work – natural enjoyment.

PRACTICE
- Do something physical in the service of the divine.
- When you derive natural enjoyment from the physical things, consider what principle you are serving in the process.

No limits

Great art has the power to open the heart. What else do we demand of it but in some way to be moved by it? Consider your own experience. One example springs to my mind.

I was visiting the Metropolitan Museum of Art in New York. One of its galleries is devoted to Dutch domestic paintings, Rembrandt included. The paintings are hung in such a way that as you approach the entrance to the gallery you see, through the doorway, a beautiful painting of a Dutch couple. It is a brilliantly executed piece of art and I stopped to admire it in detail before entering the gallery.

As I walked forward, the rest of the paintings came into view. There was a strikingly beautiful Rembrandt hanging to the right.

LANDSCAPE OF THE SOUL

Although of the same subject, it was entirely different in execution, roughly painted by comparison, seemingly dashed off when compared with the detailed care and precision evident in the other painting. There was also another noticeable difference. It seemed to speak of an entirely different level of human experience.

Easily recognized in the Rembrandt was the husband's love for his wife, in his gaze, in his protective arm around her shoulder. In her quiet demeanour was evidence of her total reciprocation. But this wasn't a formal representation of love. This was the thing itself, and being the thing itself, although entirely personal, intimate even, there was a dimension that went entirely beyond the particular. This was a portrait of love that transcended time, that transcended place.

These people were in love, and love fills the whole painting. This is a portrait of love by a painter who is in love with his subject, and his love informs every brush stroke. Although he stands as an outsider, Rembrandt is not separate from his subject. He has a complete understanding of it, because he is a lover too. He gazes open-heartedly. He paints open-heartedly, and we who go to view the painting have our hearts opened in turn. Caught in the spirit of love, all of us are linked. The husband and wife are at one, Rembrandt is at one with them, and we are one with them all. This is our contribution to the creative process.

My first impression told me that the painting I had been looking at previously was complete and contained within its frame, but that the Rembrandt had no limits. It seemed to go on for ever, and it had no limits because it evoked the principle of limitless love.

There is no doubt about the physicality of a painting, but there are some paintings we wouldn't eat our supper off. They are reserved for some other purpose: feeding the soul.

PRACTICE

- We must consider what we are feeding the soul with.
- Choose food that opens the heart and nourishes the lover in us all.

Angels in the street

Have you ever noticed that, after visiting a really wonderful exhibition, you see through the eyes of the artist. You leave the gallery and the vision lingers; Madonnas are noticed everywhere and lovers in the street possess the same endlessness and timelessness that Rembrandt invests in his paintings. This doesn't just happen with paintings, either. Somebody was telling me the other day of how when she goes to a concert, she comes out somehow feeling lighter and goes round doing unusual things like stroking cats and smiling at complete strangers. She has her concerns about this untypical behaviour, but the real concern is that after a while the feeling goes, and all the usual irritation and isolation takes over. Is all this just a change of mood, or are times like this granting us a truer appreciation of things?

I've never seen hosts of angels in the streets, but after keeping the company of Giotto or Fra Angelico people do seem different. Those around you are given a vitality that does something more than agitate the mind. Beauty is to be found everywhere. Perhaps this is why Florentine women are known for their beauty. They possess nothing more than other women possess. It's just that all that Florentine artwork cleanses the senses and refines the mind, and we become far more conscious of physical beauty.

In the following extract Emily Dickinson clearly states that it's not so much a matter of it being nice, if the mood should take us, but when it comes to our long-term prospects there is an utter necessity of seeing things as they truly are and not covering them with a dull gloss of world weariness.

> *Who has not found the heaven below*
> *Will fail of it above.*
> *God's residence is next to mine,*
> *His furniture is love*

According to her, there's no chance of getting to heaven if the heaven that is laid out on the face of the earth isn't first appreciated. As human beings we have been given all that is necessary to see and appreciate such things. When she refers to 'the furniture of love' it's quite evident that her belief is that the forms of nature truly seen and fully enjoyed brings us all into immediate contact with our most profound possession, the principle of love.

PRACTICE

- Don't automatically accept that the way you see things now is by necessity the way things truly are.
- Ask yourself: 'Of what at this moment does my world consist?'
- If in the process you see the limitations you have placed upon things, whether mental or emotional, let those limitations go.

The depths

It is interesting how a painting like Rembrandt's encourages us to look beyond the surface of things into the creative depths from which it arose. According to our normal way of thinking about things 'the depths' shouldn't exist, but they do. Our experience tells us as much. It's interesting how we use this word depth which, though recognizable by the effect it has upon us, is hard to understand or express.

Often 'deep' is used with a certain irony, as if we are deluding ourselves and others in our recognition of depth, and yet when talking about a work of art that has beauty and profundity we can't help but talk about its 'depth'.

If we are used to thinking in material terms, any such talk may seem fanciful in the extreme, but Cézanne wasn't the only one to see things like this. Take, for instance, the painter Paul Klee. This is what he says about the artist's function.

Standing at his appointed place, the trunk of the tree, he does nothing other than gather and pass on what comes to him from the depths. He neither serves nor rules – he transmits.

Klee is only too certain in his own mind as to the importance of that place and the artist's relationship to it. He doesn't so much speak of it but from it. The artist, according to Klee, is the vehicle by which it might be known.

Describing the creative process, Matisse speaks of what joy it is to:

... work with my model until I have it enough in me to be able to improvise, to let my hand run while respecting the grandeur and sacredness of all living things.

For him the creation of a work of art involves a gathering of strength until he arrives at that point where the creative process begins to take on its own inherent life. By using the words 'grandeur' and 'sacredness' he makes it clear from where he thinks this work is arising – 'the depths', for these are the divine qualities he is speaking of.

In his description he starts off by using terms we can all readily understand. He works with his model. He paints his subject. What else might an artist do? He stands before his canvas, filling out its surface with colour, shade and texture. What is also understandable is his use of the word 'improvise'. He is creating the composition as he goes along. We can see his hand holding the brush, applying paint to the surface of the canvas, his eye looking up, taking in the play of colour and light, returning to the canvas to add further detail. Stimulated by his subject, he creates.

The physicality of it all is obvious – physical subject, physical artist, physical painting. If we entertain the possibility that this activity is not just physical, the words sacredness and grandeur will confirm that opinion. His words speak of what he is experiencing, of what he so potently recognizes during the whole of the creative process. These qualities can only be recognized in his subject because he possesses them within himself. They appear to arise from 'the depths'.

In failing to recognize depth, we are, inevitably, doomed to live on the surface of life, never going beneath to connect with life's inner qualities or what lies beyond that, the realm of 'light and love' as Cézanne calls it.

PRACTICE

- Find the depths in your own life. Consciously look out for the inner qualities.
- Look out for the sacredness and grandeur. Name these qualities. The more we recognize their presence the more they will appear to us.

The memory of reality

Over and over again the great artists express themselves in these terms. From the way he speaks, too, Van Gogh was amongst those people who are familiar with this universal language of the soul.

Art, although produced by man's hands, is something not created by the hands alone, but something that wells up from a deeper source out of our soul ... My sympathies in the literary as well as in the artistic field are drawn most strongly to those artists in whom I see most the working of the soul.

According to this way of thinking, if the artist is successful in expressing something of the inner content of the soul, he will awaken memory of spiritual realities in the soul of his viewers. They will share in his inspiration. This is why we find the truly great works so satisfying, so nourishing and so inspiring. They carry, as Plato declares in the Phaedrus, 'the pristine memory of reality and the unforgettable glory of Intelligible Beauty'. The art does not import anything. It arouses the memory of what already exists within us all.

But where might we start to look for these hidden depths? Matisse was certain of where to look: in all living things.

PRACTICE

- Search for them there, in all living things, whether it be in the

mystery of a distant star or the opening of a child's eye.
- Look and then look again for the inner reality that lies beneath the surface of sensory impression.

The fairest thing that we can experience

The fairest thing we can experience is the mysterious. It is the fundamental emotion that stands at the cradle of true art and true science. He who knows it not and can no longer wonder, no longer feel amazement, is as good as dead, a snuffed out candle.

This is the voice of science speaking (the words are Einstein's), the voice of true science and true art, the art and science of the soul. They echo perfectly the words of Kandinsky, one of the founding fathers of modern art. In his book *On the Spiritual in Art*, Kandinsky makes the startling statement that an artist who fails to manifest these inner qualities in his art, the qualities of the soul, is like 'a glove without a hand'.

Repeated over and over again by men and women of insight is that this place does exist. Beneath the outer surface of continual activity lies a stiller, deeper place, and that place needs to be explored. Indeed, this is not only an imperative for any practising artist, but if any of us wants to gain something more than a surface impression of life, if we want to be something more than 'a glove without a hand', we must search for those depths in every aspect of our experience of life.

Remember the people we are talking about are creative people. Their creativity is so potent because it arises from the depths. To quote Klee once more:

Art does not recreate the visible but makes visible.

Having explored all this, however, the thought must arise, 'Perhaps this is the way that these people see it because they are exceptional, geniuses. But am I exceptional? I think not.'

Maybe, but why not try thinking about this in a different way?

Rather than thinking that these people are exceptional and therefore they are more capable of taking on this exploration of the inner world, consider instead how they used what they had to start their journey and how, because of their dedication, they were given more and more understanding and the effective means of expressing it.

The great thing is to make a start, knowing that the greatness of the offering is not the important thing, but the spirit in which that offering is made is what counts. Whatever you are engaged upon, do it for the love of it, and then make your offering for the love of others. Your greatness or achievement is not the important matter. In fact, that's of no consequence at all. By making the offering out of love, it is love that people receive, and it is love alone that allows for the proper development of mankind, however that love might manifest.

PRACTICE

- Make your offering without any hope of reward.
- If rewards do come, claim nothing, but recognize and honour the source of your inspiration. This is beauty in action, unimpeded by ego.

Love is the soul of genius

This is the essential thing that we are talking of here, so do forgive me if I write a little more about genius and love and we who live our lives, geniuses in our own right, although only in a small way.

The renowned geniuses are usually considered exceptional, and they have their art and science to prove it. We may have a little less, but genius isn't particular. Genius is universal. By rubbing, the genius may appear out of a particular lamp in a very potent sort of way. In fact, according to the story of Aladdin, it's the only way it can be done, and particular people have particular aptitudes that make genius appear more readily. The power that appears in all its particularity is universal in nature, and all can access it, but only after there has been an acknowledgment of the presence of that power and some work of devotion to it.

Remembering that the purpose of this book is to consider how we might access and employ the Venus Principle, let me press the point that at the heart of genius lies love, and that if we want to develop our talents to the full we must first become lovers.

I sometimes take part in a programme which explores in words and music the creative genius of Mozart and Shakespeare. Apart from the pleasure derived from giving the audience pleasure, to spend an evening in the company of these wonderful men is a great joy. In reality the joy is derived from the love they manifest, and regardless of how well or how badly we feel we have performed, there is always a sense of transformation having taken place in all those involved, performers and audience alike. The genius has been let out of the bottle.

The programme starts with these words found in Mozart's album:

True genius without love is a thing of naught – for not great understanding alone, not imagination alone, nor both together make genius – Love! Love! Love! That is the soul of genius.

Then a little later in the programme come these lines from Shakespeare:

> *Never durst poet touch a pen to write*
> *Until his pen were tempered by love's sighs;*
>
> *O, then his lines would ravish savage ears,*
> *And plant in tyrants mild humility.*

Here is a very clear indication that love is at the heart of genius, both in its creation and its effect. Love is the unifying factor. It also overcomes the greatest obstacle of all, the tyrant that lives in our own hearts, which in its unceasing demands hardens the heart and creates separation.

When Shakespeare talks of ravishing savage ears and engender-
ing in the hearts of tyrants mild humility, he is referring to nothing
other than the operation of the powers of Venus, courtesy of the
words and music of the artist, on the power of the ego to confine
us within its limitations. But before that may be made possible,
there must come the artist's own devotion to the spirit of love.
Without that his genius is 'a thing of naught'.

PRACTICE

- Become artists in the art of life by conscious devotion to the
  spirit of love.
- When the promptings of the ego are most strong, then is the
  time, hard as it might be, to let go of all those tensions of mind
  and body that must come with its tyranny, and devote yourself
  to the spirit of love by recalling to mind her image.
- We have already spoken of how Botticelli depicted love.
  Remembering the words of the great poets is another way of
  accessing her spirit. In learning them by heart we may carry
  them with us always.

The overshadowing of the highest

There is in the Uffizi Gallery in Florence, in the room next to the
Botticelli, an early work by Leonardo, *The Annunciation*.

Like all of Leonardo's paintings it is part portrait, part landscape,
and like all Leonardo's paintings it speaks directly to the soul. It is
evident from reading his notebooks that Leonardo was scientific in
his approach when describing the physical world, but in his
portrayal of the physical he penetrates the outer surface. It is this
capability that makes him so venerated as an artist. *The Annunciation*
lends itself to a description of the inner reality, being a portrayal of
the Virgin Mary meeting the Angel Gabriel, a messenger from that
world.

This painting may be divided into two. In the foreground Mary and Gabriel are shown meeting in a garden. At the edge of this garden is a low wall, and beyond the wall is a most beautiful landscape. The two aspects of the painting mirror each other perfectly, for what is symbolized in the foreground is portrayed in the magical landscape that lies beyond. If the foreground represents a spiritual conception, 'the overshadowing of the Highest', as it is described in the Gospels, then what is beyond the wall is the physical world revealed in the same light.

Inevitably enough, all the elements are to be found consciously represented in this landscape. Earth is there in the lie of the land, water in the river flowing through the painting, and water finer still in the fine mist hovering in the air. The beautiful fire of sunlight is also to be found suffusing the whole picture. All of the elements are seen withdrawing, going back to the vanishing point where the river cuts through the hills in the background, and from the way the low light strikes the cypress trees in the foreground, even the sunlight itself seems to be coming from the same place. It is from here that all the physical elements appear to manifest.

And what of ether, said to be the element that stands at the transition between the physical and subtle worlds? Is this represented in the painting? There is a sense of ether being present, in the background, as everything vanishes into the unmanifest. The scene dissolves into the vanishing point, which is also the arising point. It is from here the whole painting not only disappears but also starts its journey of manifestation, and in its manifestation it carries with it a sense of the divine.

The events portrayed in the foreground speak of this world in symbolic terms. The landscape beyond, by Leonardo's consummate artistry and depth of vision, portrays 'the overshadowing presence of the Highest' in the very forms of creation. Using the Tuscan hills as his model, Leonardo portrays heaven laid out on the face of the earth, a landscape of the soul finding its counterpart in the play of the elements.

PRACTICE

- Don't allow your seeing to stop at the physical. Look beyond.
- By adopting a more reflective frame of mind, come to recognize 'the overshadowing of the Highest'.
- The world is not flat. In addition to the surface of things, connect with their 'height' and 'depth'.

A copy of perfection

Plato talks of how the ever-changing forms of the physical world are emblems of the eternal principles of beauty, love and joy. He claims that it is the job of the artist to bring 'all to the perfection of beauty', and this can only be done by looking within. If the artist limits himself to copying the physical world, then his art must lack true beauty, but if he sees something of the world of divine qualities then that will find its expression. Michelangelo was of exactly the same opinion. Speaking in religious terms, he says:

Good painting is but a copy of this perfection, a shadow of His pencil, a music, a melody ... Painting is the music of God, the inner reflection of his luminous perfection.

Michelangelo is describing the luminosity of the underlying perfection, indicating that his function as an artist is to penetrate the surface and portray the divine, so that we may recognize its presence. Art of this nature becomes a kind of tuning device, a means of hearing the unheard melodies that emanate from this world of the soul.

There is a music, a melody to life. Very often we lose the thread of this tune, fail to recognize its presence, and live like aliens in our own land. The function of art, of painting, of poetry, of philosophy, according to so many great traditions of wisdom, is to allow us to remember something of what has been there all along, which was with us from the beginning but has somehow been overlooked. This is the innate perfection of the Ideal. It is to this that artists with their own intuitive insight have turned time and time again. It is to this that we might turn and come to appreciate in the everyday realities of life. By so doing we may learn to enter once more this landscape of the soul.

PRACTICE

- Don't dismiss the world as being merely physical, something to manipulate for your own pleasure and ease. This is no way to love life.
- Learn to wonder at this world by recognizing its supreme intelligence and beauty.
- The world is constantly lit. It is we who live in darkness. First open your eyes and then your heart and mind and come to appreciate the luminosity of life's underlying perfection.

The inner presence

There is so much to be discovered in the sensory world of beauty, love and joy, but what is there can only begin to be recognized because the same principles exist within. The outer evokes the inner. Many of our frustrations in life arise because we try to pursue our happiness in the outer world only, whilst ignoring the inner, and yet we ignore those inner principles at our peril, for it is those principles that grant true significance to life.

I went to India in the summer to visit my husband's relations. I found myself talking to my brother-in-law about the deep satisfaction my husband derives from his sculpture, which he practises whenever he has the opportunity. He responded by saying: 'It's a way he has of touching the divine in himself. That's the source of all true satisfaction. Why practise any art if it doesn't remind you of that? Even the dancers in the street know that by dancing they have a glimpse of the divine.'

In the conversation I had with the woman who related this observation, we went on to discuss those of us who appear to lack the means, who don't have a way of connecting, who possess lives that seem to encourage anything but the seeking of those inner principles. What is true of any art is also true of the 'art of life'. In failing to develop this art we must become alienated, desperately seeking some outer satisfaction whilst remaining strangers to the landscape of our own souls.

PRACTICE

- Find those elements in your own life that grant you satisfaction, and, having found them, tend them. Don't take them for granted or, worse still, think of them only in terms of what they can do for you. Serve them.
- By sacrificing yourself to the things you love, you will discover more about yourself. This is a way of going below the surface of personal desire and claim and connecting with the inner world where beauty, love and joy exist in their fullness.

Chapter nine

The end of separation

I F LOVE OFFERS ANYTHING it offers the end of separation. If we are driven back upon ourselves in any way, if we feel isolated and alone, consider what it is that makes us feel like this. What is it that we have lost contact with, both in the world around us, in our relationships, in our general experience of life and, most importantly, in ourselves? What emotions do we carry in our hearts, and how do these emotions colour everything?

If love is not the basis of our experience, then lack of love and all that accompanies that state will rush in to cover it. When our activities become a burden, when our relationships are a source of heartache, when natural enjoyment is replaced by tension and anxiety, we know that we have lost in some way and to some measure the capacity to love. But despite the pain that must accompany this acknowledgment, it has its purpose, for it may encourage us to wonder what it is we are lacking. What is love? From where does it arise, and what is the natural outcome of love? Above all, how might we both enjoy and offer the fullness of love?

In seeking answers to these questions we are being prompted by the most deep rooted of desires. We are seeking the source of human satisfaction and ultimate happiness. It is to the principle of love, the Venus Principle, that this book is dedicated.

And speaking of dedication, the dedication of books is a beautiful thing, for it's the offering of an endeavour to another out of the acknowledgment of a debt we owe, usually the debt of affection.

This book is dedicated to my grandchildren, and it's certainly offered out of the debt of affection; more affectionate children it would be hard to imagine.

When paintings such as *The Birth of Venus* were created the idea prevailed that another kind of dedication was possible, a dedication to the gods, that in dedicating our efforts in this way, it was possible to call down celestial powers to assist us, that, by magic, these powers could be invested in the things we created, and that in the contemplation of these objects, these powers could be passed on and used to feed the human soul. Therefore, when we devote our thoughts, as we have been doing, to the memory of Venus, inevitably all that this goddess embodies is aroused within us, for although these powers are pictured by the poets as occupying some far-off place or even circling the earth in a planetary harmony, in truth they are within, waiting to be called upon.

In the last act of Shakespeare's *The Merchant of Venice*, when the conflict is over, the spirit of love that has lain behind the action of the play rises to the surface, and the whole thing becomes, in the most playful of ways, a hymn to love. The characters are full of love, and inevitably the words they speak arouse the spirit of love in their audience.

The action of the play moves, in time, from night to day, and towards the beginning of the final act Lorenzo looks up at the night sky and speaks these words to his beloved Jessica.

> *Sit, Jessica. Look how the floor of heaven*
> *Is thick inlaid with patines of bright gold:*
> *There's not the smallest orb that thou behold'st*
> *But in his motion like an angel sings,*
> *Still quiring to the young eyed cherubins.*
> *Such harmony is in immortal souls:*
> *But while this muddy vesture of decay*
> *Doth grossly close it in, we cannot hear it.*

In this poetry the issue is plainly laid before us. In becoming possessed by all things material, we are deaf to the harmony that is contained in our souls. By believing ourselves to be physical entities and not spiritual ones, the inner organs of perception, wherein lie the true power of the imagination to release the divine within us, are dormant.

In the recognition of the power of love and in doing things out of love, for the love of them, we are consciously evoking the spirit of love and allowing that spirit to imbue all those things to which we turn our minds and hands. This is catching, for in the process we allow others to reacquaint themselves with love.

In this respect the dedicating of this book to Sam is not so far from a dedication to the spirit of love; something done out of love in the spirit of love.

PRACTICE

- Carry the image of love with you in whatever form appeals to you.
- Dedicate your actions even in the midst of action. Even the briefest of acknowledgment has its effect, a smile in the direction of love.

The unity of the family

And speaking of grandchildren, I am writing this having just returned from Southern Spain where my first granddaughter was christened. My son and daughter-in-law were married with the minimum fuss in a registry office in London. It certainly wasn't a Catholic wedding nor was it much of a family affair, but the chris-tening was different. It was in Spain, and in Spain family is not something to be overlooked.

There were obstacles to overcome, however. The major one was to get a priest to carry out the ceremony. My son is not a Catholic and has no intention of becoming a Catholic. The initial difficulty that they encountered in finding a priest proved in the end to be a blessing. An old priest, a friend of the family, came out of retirement to perform the ceremony in the most simple and most beautiful of churches. It was in the industrial district of Almeria. The church's tranquillity in comparison to its surroundings was marked; it's vitality too. It was alive. We had to wait for my daughter-in-law's old nanny to arrive. She is now in her nineties and was very much an honoured guest. Whilst waiting, the priest, dressed in his freshly pressed, pure white vestments, talked about his church and the beautiful restoration that had been carried out. The walls were white. His vestments were white. The frescoes were in the colours of southern Spain – earth colours, ochre and creamy yellows, and blues, those beautiful Mediterranean blues.

At last the nanny appeared and the ceremony was carried out, most unceremoniously. The priest was old. He sat. He was a friend of the family, and he spoke like one addressing his family. Apart from the traditional formulations that the service demanded, he said something that showed his greatness of heart. Regardless of faith, Catholic, Protestant or no faith at all, the willingness to have a child christened spoke of a recognition of those divine principles that can never be entirely ignored, that serve as a measure and direction for life.

At the end of the service, before he joined the family for photographs, he gave his blessing. A blessing of this nature in these circumstances is worth a great deal. It is a blessing for the newly christened child. It is also a blessing for the whole family and serves to express the principle of love that must be at the heart of any family, whatever form it takes. If family is merely considered as an economic or social unit, then the unity of the family must inevitably be eroded or lost completely. Also lost are the family roles. We all had our part to play, from the ninety-year-old nanny to the newly christened child. There were no divisions and our respective families had expanded to embrace one another. This is the unity of the family, and celebrations of this sort are needed to be able to express this unity.

PRACTICE

- Be aware of the unity of your own family. Keep in touch.
- Find ways of serving the family, allowing a sense of family to expand ever wider, embracing all those who come within its influence.

Love is the price of love

In a state of separation it is extremely difficult to give and to receive. We are bound within a confine of our own making.

All that we have been speaking of has been devoted to opening the heart and mind to a possibility, the possibility of a life lived in the spirit of love, where every encounter we have with life, positive or negative, may be looked upon as an opportunity to practise the law of love. It is a life in which our fundamental ambition is to seek a greater opportunity for love's expression – remembering always that it is not the greatness of the deed that counts but the spirit in which it is offered. There is one requirement in all this, an awareness of the need – not our need, but of what events demand of us. Love is not love when it places on the situation a personal demand.

If we hold ourselves as individuals to be all-important, then that which the individual values – namely his own separate existence – must rule our experience of life. This is, inevitably, a life of separation and division. On one side lies Me and on the other lies the Rest, and our actions must be entirely ruled by this fundamental divide. It is full of personal desire and frustration, full of ideas about me and mine, and on every situation is inevitably placed a personal requirement.

All this has the effect of cutting us off from a full and proper appreciation of the world around us, and also from the divine qualities that lie within. These divine qualities have their peculiar expression, and we are the only ones who can express them in our own peculiar way. They are also, by nature, universal. Paradoxically, it is only by giving up the personal that the universal can come to imbue the personal with all its magnificent qualities. To rise out of a state of separation and to unite with those divine principles of beauty, love and joy, we must firstly accept they exist, deliberately bring them to mind, seek out evidence of their presence, and, in the process of embracing the universal, abandon petty and selfish concerns.

With thoughts of these principles constantly in mind, look again and again at what is presenting itself now. Think how you might serve the situation rather than taking from it. When we love something, we can't help but serve it. Likewise, when we offer selfless service, love must follow from it.

Love is the gift of oneself, and in giving we receive. Love is the true price of love, and therefore if we wish to receive love we must first seek the means of giving it.

PRACTICE

- Each of us has our own personal way of making our offering. Seek it out.
- Having found the opportunity, pay for it with love, for love is the price of love.
- When one opportunity has come, many may follow. This is to discover the abundance of life, for in giving we receive.

Meditation, remembrance and song

In all of this we are once more talking about forms of evocation and dedication. In ancient times the poets evoked the muses to assist them with composition. In fact, they believed that their contribution to the creative act was as a vehicle for the muses. If this were really the case, you would think that their poetry would be rather impersonal. Far from it, for despite using established forms, their poetry was utterly individual, and the greater they were, the more their individual genius was stamped on their verse. They dedicated themselves to the muses, and in turn the muses enabled them to fulfil themselves as poets. The muses breathed into their verse divine inspiration.

So who are these muses?

According to myth they are the daughters of Zeus, the ultimate god in the Hellenic pantheon, the personification of the bright sky, and his wife, Mnemosyne, memory. Although generally thought of as nine, originally there were only three muses: Melete, Mneme, Aoide. Translated they become Meditation, Remembrance and Song.

As such they sound more like activity than entity, indeed they sound very much like the creative process. First, through inner reflection or meditation, our memory is aroused. This memory is deep intuitive knowledge of something that lies within us rather than anything that may appear to lie outside. From this intuitive knowledge, by the aid of art, arises song – the forms of artistic endeavour.

When Shakespeare came to describe the creative act, it was a matter of 'airy nothing' finding a 'local habitation and a name'. Airy nothing in these terms is Zeus, the bright sky – space suffused by light – and out of this limitlessness arise created forms.

How is this done?

Mnemosyne, the wife of Zeus, gives us an indication. As Memory, she provides a way of arousing the knowledge we all possess. According to these ancient thinkers and all those who followed them, those who were encouraged to make their own connection, it wasn't memories of what we were doing last night, or even what we were doing at our mother's knee, that is really important. It is the memory of those divine principles lodged in each individual soul.

In this process of remembering, we are not attempting to live in some nostalgic past, where all great things were to be discovered in their pristine perfection. No, whether we like it or not, the only time for these memories to be aroused is now, and only now can they be applied in a way that is ripe for the times. In our inspired moments we are living in the light of those perfect principles in order to serve the immediate need, regardless of how imperfect the present may appear or indeed how imperfect may be our attempts.

PRACTICE

- Don't miss out on life by being possessed of memories that are dead and past redemption.
- Have memories which by their nature are to be discovered only in the present, where life is lit.

The strength comes from within

The divine world is constantly present, and when the divine qualities come within view, it's not as if they arise, it's simply that our impediments are removed and we remember. They are our own natural qualities. It is ourselves that we remember.

Often it's at times of disaster that memory is strongest. Then the divine qualities arise in the form of courage and strength to meet the desperate need of the situation:

I went to visit a friend last week who has lost her twins when six months' pregnant.

Disaster puts everything into perspective. All our clutter disappears. The little worries are no longer important.

I went to visit her not knowing what to expect. I took a few minutes quiet before I met her. Everything seemed soft, real and vibrant even within this terrible grief. It was very important to be in the moment.

Times like this show the beauty within people. I was very concerned about how she would cope, but what emerged was rock-solid strength and courage. The strength comes from within. It's like the real you. I would never have thought that after talking and crying, we could go on to look at maps and discuss holidays.

Under such circumstances as these the trivial drops away. It is the trivial that keeps us penned within petty confines, that prevents our true qualities from manifesting. But when the circumstances command a response, the situation is met quite differently. How evident this is in the observation. What is also clear is the depth of their meeting, the unity that existed between the two women.

When the woman who made the observation said that she 'took a few minutes quiet', it indicates the approach she adopted. It would seem that before she met her friend she felt she needed to come to herself, to rid herself of all those petty agitations that sustain separation and prevent the possibility of a proper meeting. In the way she describes everything as being – 'soft, real and vibrant' – it is evident that, despite the sad circumstances, her thoughts turned entirely outwards in order to serve the need of her friend. It also speaks inevitably enough of heightened awareness. In this reflective state of mind, acting out of love for her friend, not only did the physical world have a greater sense of reality, she also came to the profound conclusion that:

The strength comes from within. It's like the real you.

In circumstances like this we discover that all those things that usually possess the mind, to which we invest our identity, prevent us from making contact with what we really are. Any insight into what lies beneath the surface cannot help but generate love. Read her words again, and you'll see what I mean.

PRACTICE

- Use reflection to come to yourself by falling still and making full and proper contact with the peace to be found in the present. Act from that.

Intimations of immortality

What exactly is reflection? What is reflecting in what? In so many of the great philosophical traditions there is the concept of 'the mirror of the mind' or 'the mirror of the soul', and in this mirror is reflected both the forms of creation and the light of consciousness – that fundamental power which allows us to recognize anything. The light of consciousness is, in the normal run of things, sucked into all those concerns that captivate our minds. We are usually so involved with them that we forget the light which illuminates it all, the light of consciousness. When we reflect, however, we are taking our attention away from all those possessing concerns to rest in the inner light.

This light is cool and clear, calm and all embracing. This light of consciousness is the very substance of love. Although it illuminates everything that arises in our minds as individuals, this is not an individual consciousness. Consciousness has no limits. Therefore, when in a reflective state we act from this consciousness, it is the sense of unity that we experience, and although we see creation in all its variety, perhaps more vividly than we normally experience it, there is also an awareness that underlying the variety is unity.

The following is an extract from Wordsworth, writing as he often does, reflectively. He speaks of consciousness as 'the mighty being':

> It is a beauteous evening, calm and free;
> The holy time is quiet as a nun
> Breathless with adoration; the broad sun
> Is sinking down in tranquillity;
> The gentleness of heaven is on the sea.
> Listen! the mighty being is awake
>
> And doth with his eternal motion make
> A sound like thunder – everlastingly.

Times like this have their appeal. Many of us desire to experience the greater depth and happiness that are associated with such times.

Are there not moments in all our memories just as vivid as this, moments that contain more than a touch of bliss?

According to Plato, it is the function of both poetry and philosophy to awaken memory, memory of the supreme happiness that transcends time and place. He claims that although the soul has journeyed forth and finds her home in time and space, she always carries with her the memory of her own innate reality. It is not for nothing that Wordsworth called the collection of poems from which this extract was drawn, *Intimations of Immortality*. By reflection we may illuminate those eternal principles of beauty, love and joy, and by so doing allow them to become our reality.

PRACTICE

- Adopt a more reflective state of mind.
- Constantly come to yourself. Rest in the light of your own inner consciousness rather than being sucked into the next big involvement.
- Treat life as a journey of self-discovery, not as a soap opera – or, if you like soap operas, enjoy them as spectacles, remembering that reality lies elsewhere.

A hut in the mountains

We often associate moments of real reflective insight with a particular place or a particular kind of occasion. There's certainly a great joy to be had in seeking the beauties of nature, whether by the sea as Wordsworth describes it or in the mountains. Wordsworth often uses the Lake District, where he was born, as a setting for his reflective poetry and often talks about his desire for solitude:

> ... by the margin of the trembling lake,
> Beneath the gloomy hills I went
> In solitude.

Men and women often seek seclusion away from the business of life. This certainly has its benefits, but also its dangers. There is another possibility.

A woman made an observation recently of how, whilst she was

living in Switzerland, she had a persistent desire to have a hut in the mountains. In this hut she and her husband would find rest and repose, peace and quiet away from the turmoil of everyday life: the television, the newspapers and all those things that fill the mind with agitation. The problem was that the desire for 'a hut in the mountains' became so strong that it clouded everything else with a sense of dissatisfaction.

This went on until one day she realized that her 'hut in the mountain' could be found within. It was a reservoir of peace and bliss that she could turn to always.

This is not a place of escape but a place of renewal. By casting aside for a while the involvements of life, it allows us to appreciate that behind all these involvements, all this activity and agitation, there lies a place of stillness and rest. It is in the memory of the unified state of consciousness that we may come to appreciate that all the movements of life arise out of this stillness and rest, and, when their course is run, will return to them. Whilst we are in contact with this place, all the business of life may be dealt with compassionately and intelligently.

PRACTICE

- Love arises when separation goes.
- In resting in our own inner state of unity, the capability of loving our neighbours isn't something we are commanded to do, but something which by necessity arises.
- Let the divisions disappear by resting in that which has no division.

At the root of it all

The end of separation is not something we are seeking but something that is already achieved, if only we knew it. Love is not an emotion that we would like to experience but exists as a continuous substratum to life, if only we knew it.

The physicist Sir Arthur Eddington, in a fascinating essay called *Mind Stuff*, makes the following claim:

Our yet deeper feelings are not of ourselves alone, but are glimpses of a reality transcending the narrow limits of our particular consciousness – that the harmony and beauty of the face of Nature is, at root, one with the gladness that transfigures the face of man.

We have already considered the possibility that we can only discover the beauty without because we have beauty within. Notice the great beauty of his words as he acknowledges this:

... the harmony and beauty of the face of Nature is, at root, one with the gladness that transfigures the face of man.

Such an observation arises out of an appreciation of the underlying unity of which we may gain glimpses. This is speaking of that state where the division of the so-called subjective and so-called objective worlds breaks down, where we are not separate from everything around us but part of a transcendent totality. He is speaking of those profound memories sown in every man's soul. It is important that we hold ideas like this before the mind, for they stir those memories, not only of harmony and beauty but of the love out of which these words so evidently arise.

PRACTICE

• Make it the major purpose of your life to connect with the light of consciousness in order that the divine qualities which are your own qualities may form your central experience of life.

Progress being made

When we see things from our own separate stance, everything must be seen in a divided way, and we end up manipulating events to serve some private end. This is a hard frame of mind to change.

The principles that we have been exploring are beyond this

private frame of mind. Although experienced personally, they are universal and possessed by all. When we start seeing like this and thinking like this, everything changes.

In the opening chapter we noted how Max Planck, exploring the question 'Where is Science Going?', explained the way science encourages a love of truth and reverence and how in our ever more profound exploration of what appears to be the outer nature of things, we come to an ever deeper awareness of that which quests, what he describes as the 'mystery of our own being'. This mystery can be nothing other than the conciousness that empowers it all.

In an interview, he returned to this theme:

Science cannot solve the ultimate mystery of nature. And that is because, in the last analysis, we are part of nature, and, therefore part of the mystery we are trying to solve.

Music and art are, to an extent, also attempts to solve or at least express the mystery. But to my mind, the more we progress with either, the more we are brought into harmony with all nature itself.

When 'the ultimate mystery of nature' is approached, the differences disappear. It spells out the end of separation. This doesn't mean, however, the demise of the individual. It does mean, though, the end of the individual grasping after things, seeking to possess that which, if the truth were known, is possessed all along. We are, after all, part of nature. No one could deny that. True progress always involves a recognition of this fact. How else can we advance in understanding if we don't in some way come into tune with the laws of nature, which are the laws by which we operate at every level? When such an approach is made, what is experienced is the fading away of separation, of duality giving way to unity, and with this arises a sense of harmony and an awareness of love's totality.

PRACTICE

• When you find yourself being driven into a corner by your attempts to manipulate events to serve some personal end,

abandon this private agenda.
- Bring to mind the mystery that holds us all. This offers another solution, which, as it arises out of unity, must have its own sense of rightness and harmony, of progress being made.

Everything has me ...

The desire to express 'the ultimate mystery of nature' was something known to the painter Winifred Nicholson. She beautifully expresses what arises from being 'brought into harmony with all nature itself'. Living in St Ives, it was the beauty of the North Cornwall coastline in all its changing moods from which she drew her inspiration. Not only was she aware of the world of constant change, she was also conscious of being in harmony with nature regardless of its state.

I don't want anything in the world – I just like existing every minute, and watching things coming and things going, and then coming again, like storms and sunshine and then storms again. I don't want anything at all for the simple reason that I have everything, or rather, which is the same thing, everything has me ...

The sense that in giving up our desires we become at one with what life is offering now is very evident in what she says. She wants nothing because she has everything.

Desire is always to do with something to be obtained in the future. When the mind is fixed on that, there is not only an inherent dissatisfaction with what is being presented now, there is also an inevitable division: me and that out there from which I hope to obtain what I desire.

In her description this division has given way to a state of contentment and the recognition that, as Max Planck discovered, in the final analysis, 'we are part of nature'.

PRACTICE
- Just because we have individuality, it doesn't mean that we have to live in separation. Every time you feel yourself creating your own state of separation, cut out the cut off state and give of yourself.

- After you have given of yourself, ask yourself whether you have greater happiness or less by having done so.

Not just the molecules

Depth of insight and a sense of unity often accompany each other. We have spoken of the effects of walking in space. Here is another insight from space, one that directly recognizes the unity of matter. This time it is the voice of Edgar D. Mitchell, an astronaut on Apollo 14.

We can see the earth set against the background of billions of stars and galaxies and clusters of galaxies.

I had the experience of recognizing that it's all connected – that it is not, as we in science had tended to believe, a cosmic accident; it's all not that way at all – that the molecules of my body and the molecules of the space craft were manufactured in the furnaces of ancient stars billions of years ago. Everything was part of this process that created us, and that there is a connection between all of it; and that it's an intelligent universe, not just a piece of inanimate matter floating around.

Unity of matter certainly, but notice also his final observation about an intelligent universe. Out of a sense of the unity of matter comes an insight into the unity of intelligence. It wasn't just the molecules of his body that were forged in the furnaces of ancient stars. His own intelligence was there too.

PRACTICE

- Don't be overwhelmed by fanciful nonsense or fool yourself into believing the impossible. However, insights do arise, and we should value and remember them, but not claim them as some kind of personal possession.

An expression of something timeless

But enough of science. Let's instead return to poetry. I remember when I was 17 standing outside the public library where I was working at the time, having a conversation with one of my fellow librarians. He asked me what I really wanted to do. Out of nowhere came the words, 'I want to teach something about the beauty of great poetry.' Now these weren't desires I had ever entertained before. I had dabbled, but this ... I thought at the time: 'Where did that come from?' Later I dismissed it as nonsense, but the fact that I am writing about it now, that I still remember, says something. Looking back there comes a realization that even though the things I've done in life have been quite varied, in one way or another they have all served that same desire. So do forgive me if I return to a poetic theme.

It is, in fact, the theme that the whole of this book is devoted to, the birth of Venus, and how we might access the principle of love within us. After all, it has been made clear, I hope, that you can't be a poet without being a lover. What is also evident, I hope, is that as soon as you become a lover you can't help but be a poet. And, judging from what has been included here, even scientists have been known to burst into song. This is what the muses do for you: meditation, memory, song – song in the form of word or deed or both.

And if it is poetry, let us look at the most profound of poetical ideas: platonic love.

> *Let me not to the marriage of true minds*
> *Admit impediments. Love is not love*
> *Which alters when it alteration finds,*
> *Or bends with the remover to remove.*
> *Oh no, it is an ever fixed mark*
> *That looks on tempests and is never shaken;*
>
> *It is the star to every wandering bark,*
> *Whose worth's unknown, although his height be taken.*

Love's not time's fool, though rosy lips and cheeks
Within his bending sickle's compass come;
Love alters not with his brief hours and weeks,
But bears it out even to the edge of doom;
If this be error and upon me proved,
I never writ, nor no man ever loved.

This is *Sonnet 116*, one of the most loved of all Shakespeare's poems. If you are in any doubt about the matter, let me assure you that it is a love poem. It describes the nature of true love as opposed to those passing affections which often go by that name. It describes the constancy of love that is not bound by a life time; in fact, it's not bound by time at all. It describes love as an eternal principle – not something out there beyond our experience, but something immediately to hand, as immediate as life itself

But what is this thing called platonic love of which this poem is a clear expression?

I feel very conscious that I have throughout the whole of this book been exploring platonic love without once making a proper attempt at a definition. Maybe that's all to the good. By approaching things obliquely we are laying down lines that do more than provide words to describe words but help evoke the thing itself, in the same way as the words of the poets do. But having said this, an attempt at a definition must be made.

In doing so I will quote the man whom I have often referred to in this book, Marsilio Ficino, head of the Platonic Academy of Florence, who did more than any other to relaunch the idea that came to be known as platonic love. In his translations, commentaries and letters, he helped to open up the spiritual essence of the classical world to a Renaissance audience. He defined platonic love in these terms:

The spiritual love for another human being that is but a disguised love of the soul for its own eternal being.

PRACTICE

- Begin to look at the things you love as the expression of something timeless. It is so easy to think of them all as being temporary. After all, are we not, the enjoyers of these things, temporary? Believing that we are, it is easy enough to treat things timeless as if bound by the limitations of our individual lives and everything we want from our lives. These are beliefs that will inevitably lead to frustration, for if we believe we are bound by time, then everything is taken from us when our time is come.

    If we regard the things we love as timeless, it is their timelessness and our timelessness we will begin to enjoy.

What price any of these?

Look for the timelessness in things, and in the process find your own timelessness. Learn to love things as an expression of these timeless principles.

Let me give you an example of what I mean.

I went to a private view recently. The works were called 'easel paintings' but were, in fact, large three-dimensional reliefs cast in aluminium. There were, of course, no prices on anything, so I asked what the going price was. They were hundreds of thousands of dollars each.

I was standing in morning assembly the following day looking at the boys I teach, when the thought came to mind: 'What price any one of these?' That may appear a trite question, but its effect was far from trite. It allowed me to connect with the incredible intelligence that was everywhere. I could see each of the boys bathed in the light of this intelligence. All their animation, all their awareness was entirely dependent on the presence of this intelligence.

In educational circles there is often talk about intelligence, and we are forever measuring the product of intelligence, but intelligence in the abstract is not something much discussed. We are aware of the the result of intelligence, but the thing itself is another matter.

Intelligence in its purity is not in any way confined to this brain or that. Standing in assembly it was evident that intelligence was not confined in any way at all. It was out there filling the chapel with its brilliance. It was something that contained us all, that would still be there long after all of us were gone, teachers and pupils alike. It was, of course, profoundly beautiful and of immense value. It wasn't just the brilliant pupils who were brilliant. Everything was invested with timeless intelligence.

In one of his letters, Ficino writes:

It was the chief work of the divine Plato ... to reveal the principle of unity in all things, which is called appropriately the One itself. He also asserted that in all things there is one truth, that is the light of the One itself ...

Its splendour shines in every individual thing according to its nature and is called grace and beauty; and where it shines more clearly, it especially attracts those who are watching, stimulates those who think, and catches and possesses those who draw near to it.

This ray compels them to revere its splendour more than all else, as if it were a divine spirit, and once their former nature has been cast aside, to strive for nothing else but to become this splendour.

The Letters of Marsilio Ficino, Vol. 1

PRACTICE

- Work towards the end of separation by serving the unifying principle of timeless intelligence, however it might manifest.
- Be one who watches and thinks and seeks to unite.

Who is this mysterious woman?

In the *Symposium* Socrates talks of his own teacher. Her name is Diotima. We don't know who this mysterious person is, but we do know what her name means – Blessed by Zeus – and we do know that she is wise. Her words tell us this much. Wisdom, as far as Socrates is concerned, is not to be judged by how much you claim to know. Socrates himself was judged by the Delphic Oracle – the final authority when it came to wisdom for those ancient Greeks – to be the wisest man in Athens because he claimed to know nothing. Wisdom is more to do with the capacity to enter ever more deeply into that world of divine principles. Over the entrance to the Oracle was the most famous of all philosophic commands: 'Know thyself.' To Socrates, self-knowledge was all important.

I must first know myself, as the Delphian inscription says; to be curious of that which is not my concern while I am in ignorance of my own self would be ridiculous.

PLATO, *Phaedrus* 229E

The state of wisdom is attained by entering ever more deeply into the region of the pure and the unchanging. What is to be found there is who we really are; not that person of a thousand involvements, who is forever carving out for himself some kind of claim. In reality, we are something quite different.

Socrates was devoted to beauty and love, and it is of beauty and love in all its unchangeableness and purity that Diotima finally speaks. She says that love exists 'in an eternal oneness', that all lovely things enjoy an aspect of this 'inviolable whole'. She goes on to say that, 'under the influence of true love', those who come to recognize the unity of beauty are 'not far from the end'.

The discovery that under the influence of true love beauty is not far from the end is a state of wisdom, for 'the end' to which she refers can only be one end: self-knowledge.

In self-knowledge there is an awareness of the unity that underlies all the seeming perplexities, conflicts, divisions and separations that can dominate our lives. In this discovery, not only do we enter into a fuller relationship with everything around us, we are no longer separated from ourselves.

When we experience love of any kind, that which is closest to our hearts, that which in truth we are, forces its way to the surface, and the principle of unity to which Plato devoted his life enters our immediate experience. It may be fleeting. Ownership and claim have been long practised. But if we are to discover more about who we really are, if we are to gain anything of the true happiness that comes with self-knowledge, then we must be like Socrates and become devoted to love.

Perhaps Diotima is Venus by another name. If this is so, why not be like Socrates, and enter into a dialogue? After all, this mysterious person is no stranger. She is our own true nature.

PRACTICE

- Enter into a dialogue with the principle of love by continually calling her to mind, by laying aside all those factors in life that divide us up and separate us out, by creating space enough to let her in.

The flight from the alone to the alone

At the outset of this book we talked about how of all the powers that dominate our hearts and minds, none is more deeply sought after nor more deeply missed than love, of how we long to receive love, and long to give it. And of how when we consider what is of central importance in our lives, from which we derive our happiness, the inevitable conclusion must be that it is nothing else than love.

The purpose of this book is to encourage a deeper look at this fundamental need that we all possess and consider how we might work towards its expression, for it is only in this way that we can come to understand love's unified grandeur.

In the normal course of things we will undoubtedly discover something of love's power. It comes to us as if by chance. In this book, however, we are not discussing chance encounters, but how to develop a full and ultimately satisfying relationship with the principle of love. It is in this way that Plato claims we may care for the soul, not only care for, but allow her to find her expression, and, in the process, nourish us and all those with whom we come in contact.

At his trial Socrates stated that his purpose was to bring to his fellow men an understanding that their overriding duty was to care for the soul, placing that concern above any other. Without this devotion we become obsessed by that which must come to pass. This is a life full of desire and fear. It is a life in which we are for ever grasping after things and, having grasped them, are fearing for their loss. It is a life in which the one thing we will assuredly lose is any knowledge of the underlying totality of love.

Care for the soul is achieved by awakening to the fullness and glory of love, and by doing so discovering life's beauty and fulfilment.

The Platonic philosopher Plotinus called the whole process we have been exploring 'the flight from the alone to the Alone', the rising out of separation and isolation to live in the all-oneness of love.

We do have this impression that we are on our own, and even in the midst of friends it can be an overwhelming impression, but the truth of the matter is that we are at one and not alone. It is only the belief in our own isolation that makes us certain of its existence. The fact that everyone else appears to hold the same belief further reinforces our impression, but love overcomes all this. When love is experienced, everything is seen quite differently. Why do we value love so highly? Because by the power of love reality is revealed, and we come to know how things really are.

Conclusion

With the birth of Venus comes an intuitive awareness of the soul's proper dimension. This is why under the influence of love, life is experienced in all its fullness. But the gods don't come unless invited, and nobody ever learnt to love in theory. Let me therefore encourage you to use the insights to be found in this book, to reflect and practise.

Apart from Ficino, the person I have quoted most extensively is Shakespeare. This is not surprising as his work is imbued with all that we have been exploring. I have used lines from *Sonnet 29* elsewhere, but it makes a fitting conclusion and I make no apology for including it in full here. What it describes doesn't arise entirely by chance, despite Shakespeare's claim to the contrary. It is about the flight from the alone to the Alone, from separation to the total unity of love, the final source of human happiness.

> *When in disgrace with Fortune and men's eyes,*
> *I all alone beweep my outcast state,*
> *And trouble deaf heaven with my bootless cries,*
> *And look upon myself and curse my fate,*
> *Wishing me like to one more rich in hope,*
> *Featur'd like him, like him with friends possess'd,*
> *Desiring this man's art, and that man's scope,*
> *With what I most enjoy contented least;*
> *Yet in these thoughts my self almost despising,*
> *Haply I think on thee, and then my state,*
> *(Like to the lark at break of day arising*
> *From sullen earth) sings hymns at heaven's gate,*
> *For thy sweet love remembered such wealth brings,*
> *That then I scorn to change my state with kings.*